Historical Sketches
of the
HOLSTON VALLEYS

❖TENNESSEE❖

Thomas W. Preston

HERITAGE BOOKS
2008

HERITAGE BOOKS
AN IMPRINT OF HERITAGE BOOKS, INC.

Books, CDs, and more—Worldwide

For our listing of thousands of titles see our website
at
www.HeritageBooks.com

A Facsimile Reprint
Published 2008 by
HERITAGE BOOKS, INC.
Publishing Division
100 Railroad Ave. #104
Westminster, Maryland 21157

Cover illustration: typical frontier fort and stockade, of similar
construction to that of Fort Patrick Henry at Kingsport.

International Standard Book Numbers
Paperbound: 978-0-7884-0721-5
Clothbound: 978-0-7884-7472-9

THIS BOOK
IS RESPECTFULLY DEDICATED
TO THE
DAUNTLESS FRONTIERSMEN
WHO BLAZED THE
TRAIL OF CIVILIZATION
THROUGH
WILDERNESS AND DANGER
TO THEIR
IMMORTAL GLORY AND CREDIT

THE AUTHOR

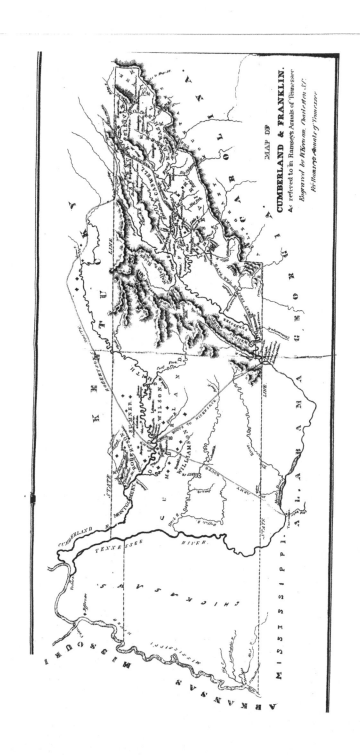

MAP OF
CUMBERLAND & FRANKLIN.
As referred to in Ramsey's Annals of Tennessee
Engraved for N.Vernon. Charleston. S.C.
for Ramsey's Annals of Tennessee

CONTENTS

LIST OF ILLUSTRATIONS

Publishers' Foreword

GOVERNMENT statistics show that Kingsport is in the very center of the Anglo-Saxon population of America and that inhabitants of the Holston Valleys are ninety-eight per cent American born, pure Anglo-Saxon stock.

In many instances the educational facilities of the Appalachian highlands are very limited, yet we have learned through our experiences during the four years since the establishment of our organization in Tennessee that the inborn intelligence of the boys and girls of the Holston Valleys is most remarkable.

The willingness of the youth from these highlands, their adaptability, earnestness and loyalty have won our admiration and constant commendation. Their potential possibilities are amazing. If, in retrospection, we allow our minds to wander backward for a century and a half and visualize the hardy ancestry from which this generation has sprung, it is easily understood.

The Holston Valleys have a historical background unsurpassed in the United States. Cut off from the Atlantic seaboard by the Appalachian Mountains, these hardy Scotch-Irish pioneers carried to a successful conclusion three campaigns that had far-reaching effect on the ultimate destiny of the nation.

These three important events were the battle of Kings' Mountain, the battle of Point Pleasant and the conquest of the Northwestern Territory by George Rogers Clark. In these sketches, these, as well as many other activities of historical interest, have been recounted and explained.

Events described herein have all been previously recorded in print. It is to be regretted that the original editions were all limited and of a character to make impossible proper preservation for posterity. The events chronicled in this little volume are but a few of the most outstanding incident to this section. There are many more just as interesting.

It is our purpose to publish at intervals

other titles dealing with this abundantly historical section of America. It is our hope that readers of these offerings may gain an intimate understanding of the accomplishments, virtues and hardships of those redoubtable pioneers—the pure Anglo-Saxon Americans—now a vanishing people.

The Publishers.

December, 1926.

ACKNOWLEDGMENT

The following books and authors have been freely consulted. Due acknowledgment and appreciation is hereby given.

DROPPED STITCHES IN TENNESSEE HISTORY . *John Allison*
NOTABLE SOUTHERN FAMILIES . . . . *Zella Armstrong*
SKETCHES OF VIRGINIA . . . . *William H. Foote*
HISTORY OF TENNESSEE . . . . *John Haywood*
LOST STATE OF FRANKLIN . . . . *Samuel C. Williams*
DUNMORE'S WAR . . . . *Thwaite & Kellog*
THE WINNING OF THE WEST . . . . . . *Theodore Roosevelt*
ANNALS OF TENNESSEE . . . . *J. G. M. Ramsey*
HISTORIC SULLIVAN . . . . *Oliver Taylor*
HISTORY OF SOUTHWEST VIRGINIA . . . . . *L. P. Summers*
KINGS MOUNTAIN & ITS HEROES . . . *Lyman C. Draper*
THE KINGS MOUNTAIN MEN . . . . *Kate K. White*
MIDDLE NEW RIVER SETTLEMENT . *David E. Johnston*
THE PASSING OF THE GREAT RACE . . . . *Madison Grant*
CLARK'S CONQUEST OF THE ILLINOIS *Consul W. Butterfield*
HANDBOOK OF AMERICAN INDIANS . *Frederick W. Hodges*
OLD VIRGINIA AND HER NEIGHBORS . . . . . . *John Fiske*
DANIEL BOONE . . . . *Reuben G. Thwaite*
THE CAMPBELL FAMILY . . . . *Margaret J. Pilcher*
BOONE AND THE WILDERNESS ROAD . *H. Addington Bruce*
LETTERS OF THOMAS JEFFERSON . . . . . . *Thomas Jefferson*
VIRGINIA, ITS HISTORY AND ANTIQUITIES . . . . . . *Howe*
A CENTURY OF DISHONOR . . . . *H. H.*
HISTORY OF KENTUCKY . . . . *Lewis Collins*
HISTORY OF KENTUCKY . . . . *John Filson*
THE FILSON CLUB, LOUISVILLE, KENTUCKY, FOR THE
    USE OF PHOTOGRAPHS OF BOONE, ETC.
THE DAVID CAMPBELL CHAPTER OF THE DAUGHTERS
    OF AMERICAN REVOLUTION FOR THE USE OF MAP
    PLATES USED IN REPRINT OF ANNALS OF TENNESSEE
UNITED STATES FORESTRY DEPARTMENT
    Samuel R. Broadbent, District Supervisor of Unaka Forest
J. M. PHIPPS   COL. SAMUEL L. KING   A. I. HAYS

Foreword

THE fifteenth century was barren of scientific or nautical information and even educated minds had a grotesque conception of the geography of the world at that time. Superstition was rampant and it was current belief that the earth was flat and that those who ventured too far afield would fall over the edge into unknown space. A study of some of the maps of that period makes the discovery of America a remarkable achievement. Despite the lack of nautical information, however, the fifteenth century developed a type of mariner whose intrepidity knew no danger, and whose zeal for discovery knew no distance. Dr. John Fiske, the eminent historian, says: "American archeology is of vital importance for the general study of the evolution of human society." This being true, it is fitting that we go back to the very earliest inhabitants of this continent in recording the history of so wonderful and historical a section as that surrounding the city of Kingsport.

When the Spanish and the English first landed on the continents of North and South America they found them inhabited by a race of people totally dissimilar to any branch of the human family then known. These early explorers encountered numerous tribes of Indians in every section that was visited. These various tribes while similar in many respects had diverse customs and languages. It has been established by scientific investigation that the American Indian belongs to the Mongolian family of the human race, but his migration to the American continent is still shrouded in mystery. There are more than twenty-five hundred tribal names mentioned in the "Handbook of American Indians" published by the Bureau of American Ethnology. None of these tribes, with possibly one or two exceptions, possessed any considerable degree of civilization.

Scientists are agreed upon the extreme antiquity of the earth, and the average individual is becoming better informed as to its geological construction and the ethnology of the peoples who have dwelt on it for unknown centuries. This progress has been made despite the fact that recorded history only traces back some sixty centuries. Geologists have established as a fact that the continents of North America and Asia were at one time united. The accepted theory is therefore very probable, that the first inhabitants of America crossed over from Asia by way of Alaska in prehistoric days.

Numerous discoveries have been made showing that this country was inhabited by human beings in the latter glacial age, which ended some fifty thousand years ago. Further research has revealed that the North American Eskimo is probably the lineal descendant of the cave man of the Pleistocene caves of western Europe. When we begin to delve in antiquity our minds are apt to become confused and it is hard to realize that the seas, continents and even the climates of the world as we know them have been just the reverse in centuries gone by. It requires quite a mental effort to visualize the British Isles as once having been united to the mainland and inhabited by a people similar to our Eskimos, or our own beautiful Holston Valley as having been the home of the mastodon, the saber-toothed tiger and the cave bear. The anthropologist has proved by recent discoveries that the American Indian dwelt on American soil for a long time and that there was no connection between this people and the Old World races for a period of twenty thousand years before the coming of the Europeans. Despite the diversity of tribes, customs and semicivilization they are all of the same origin and are entitled to be designated as belonging to the great American red race.

The American Indian had few vices and many virtues, and had he been treated with any reasonable degree of fairness and kindness would doubtless have welcomed the white man to his country and divided his all with him. Owing to a nomadic life and living in the open, contagious diseases were practically unknown among the Indians. Their physical endurance has probably never been surpassed by any other people and their bravery in both the hunt and in battle was unquestioned. They had no domestic animals such as the horse, cow, sheep and hog. The Indians subsisted principally on game, wild fruit, berries and roots, but they gave to the world one cereal plant which did much to sustain the early pioneers and explorers and hastened the settling of the new country. Indian corn had an important part in the development of the Colonies and is gradually becoming one of the important life-sustaining cereals throughout the entire world.

SKETCH ONE
The Cherokee Indians

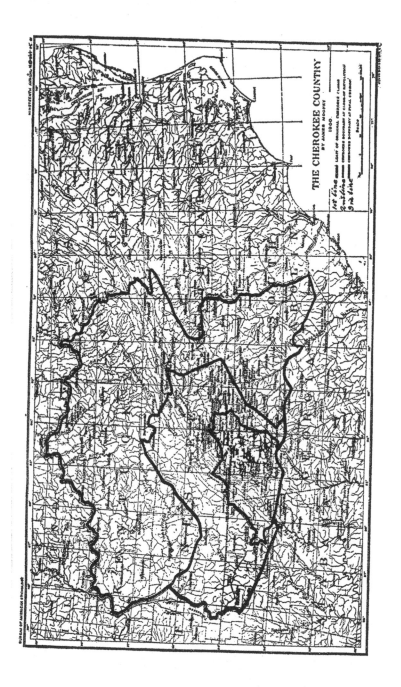

THE CHEROKEE COUNTRY
BY JAMES MOONEY
1900

1st Line —— LIMIT OF ORIGINAL CHEROKEE CLAIM
2nd Line ——— CHEROKEE BOUNDARY AT CESSION REVOLUTION
3rd Line ——— CHEROKEE BOUNDARY AT FINAL CESSION

Scale

The Cherokee Indians

THE valleys of the Holston, or what is termed the Kingsport territory, was at one time inhabited by the Cherokees. This tribe is described in the "Handbook of American Indians" as

A powerful detached tribe of the Iroquoyian family, formerly holding the whole mountain region of the South Alleghanies, in Southwestern Virginia, Western North Carolina and South Carolina, North Georgia, East Tennessee and Northeast Alabama.

Many centuries ago the Holston Valley was inhabited by a race of Indians having some slight civilization. This tribe was defeated and driven out by the Cherokees who took possession of the entire Holston Valley and established many permanent villages.

In 1765 the Confederacy of the Six Nations inaugurated the most extensive invasion that had probably ever been undertaken within the limits of what are now the boundaries of the United States. Organizing, in the vicinity of the Great Lakes, the largest band of warriors that had perhaps ever assembled on this continent, they swept with irresistible fury over the Mississippi Valley and as far east as the Blue Ridge Mountains. Many small tribes in their pathway were exterminated and even the valiant Cherokees were compelled to fall back south of the Tennessee and into the Carolinas.

Although this vast territory east of the Ohio River was conquered by the Confederacy of the Six Nations it was never permanently occupied by them. This left the Holston Valley from the mouth of Clinch River to the Blue Ridge Mountains without permanent inhabitants. Unhampered by the destructive hand of man, this vast territory became a paradise for wild beasts and game of every description. For one hundred years prior to the visit of the first explorers herds of buffalo roamed the valleys, while countless deer, black bear and wild turkeys held domain over the uplands. It was a veritable paradise for the hunter and was frequently visited by bands of Cherokees, Shawnees and other tribes. This no mans land was the scene of frequent battles between the Chero-

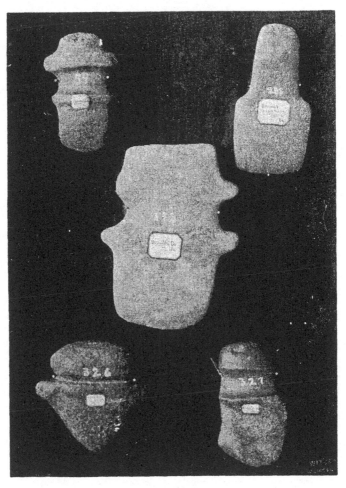

INDIAN RELICS—I. AXEHEADS AND SHOVEL (238)
From collection of Joe D. Taylor, Bristol, Tenn.,
containing 30,000 pieces

kees and other hunting tribes. The Cherokees were a brave and valiant nation and their warriors frequently went forth to battle just for the sake of testing their prowess and accumulating additional scalps.

The first contact between the Cherokees and the white man was with the expedition of De Soto, in 1540. This ruthless leader probably penetrated as far north as southwestern Virginia. With cruelty, murder and destruction he swept relentlessly through all of the Indian tribes from the Seminoles of Florida to the Chickasaws of west Tennessee. His fiendish treatment of the Cherokees engendered that distrust which burst into flame one hundred years later and was responsible to a considerable extent for the hostilities between the Cherokees and the settlers on the Holston.

From the very discovery of America it was the policy of the Spanish explorer and colonist to take possession of the new country, in the name of their king and to despoil it of its wealth regardless of the rights of the Indians. In many instances this was also the policy of our ancestors, the English, and also of the French in Canada and the Mississippi Valley.

Despite this policy of despoiling the Indians of their lands and precious metals, as practiced in Mexico and Peru, the spiritual welfare of the native tribes was a source of deep concern to the colonizing nations. Both Spain and France made it a governmental policy to foster the Christianization and civilization of the red men. The earliest missionary work among the Cherokees was that of the mysterious Christian Priber at Tellico in east Tennessee, in 1736. In 1804 Rev. Gideon Blackburn established a Presbyterian mission school among the Cherokees in east Tennessee. This school flourished for several years but finally failed for lack of funds. In 1759 the Cherokees realizing that the encroachments of the white settler would ultimately destroy their hunting grounds and deprive them of their means of sustenance started on the warpath. They were encouraged and abetted by the French in the Mississippi Valley. For nearly forty years they continued to harass the settlers, and peace was not established until 1794 when they realized that they had no chance of driving the white man back of the mountains. During the period of hostilities they had established their principal settlements in northern Georgia and along the Tennessee line. From controlling a vast empire that now constitutes several states, by the beginning of the nineteenth century they were confined to a small territorial limit south of the Tennessee River. This was due to the persistent encroachments of the white settlers and the violation of numerous treaties by the United States government.

In 1820 the Cherokees had become partially civilized and were prosperous. They had established a government fashioned after that of the United States. One of their number, Sequoya, of mixed blood, had invented a Cherokee alphabet and they were well on the road to both civilization and culture. Helen Hunt Jackson referring to the Cherokees in "A Century of Dishonor" says, "There is no instance in all history of a race of people passing in so short a space of time from the barbarous stage to the agricultural and civilized." At the height of their prosperity gold was discovered in northern Georgia, within the boundaries of the Cherokee nation. The quest and desire for gold has aroused the cupidity of mankind

since the beginning of history, and the more
civilized he becomes the more avaricious his
nature. With the discovery of gold in their
reservation, a powerful agitation was begun
by white speculators for the removal of the
Cherokees west of the Mississippi. After
years of ceaseless struggle they were forced
to surrender to the dominating policy of
"might is right" and on Dec. 29, 1835, they
sold their remaining territory and agreed to
remove to the lands allotted to them west
of the Father of Waters. This unwilling
exodus was accomplished in the winter of
1838–39. The long journey was made on
foot and the emigrants were goaded on by a
military command of United States soldiers.
A number of prominent men from east Tennessee were a part of the military guard under
General Winfield Scott. The hardships of
the journey were so great that one-fourth of
their number perished before reaching the
Mississippi and 311 more were drowned in a
steamboat accident in crossing the river. The
treatment of the Cherokees and their enforced removal from the land of their forefathers in the beautiful mountains of east
Tennessee and western North Carolina finds

INDIAN RELICS—II. PIPES AND BEAD NECKLACES
From collection of Joe D. Taylor, Bristol,
containing 30,000 pieces

a strong analogy in the Turkish persecution of the Armenians, Greeks and Syrians one hundred years later. By some strange working of the law of compensation the very land to which they were so unwillingly transported, in what is at present the state of Oklahoma, has developed one of the richest oil fields on the continent. The western Cherokees are now, per capita, one of the wealthiest peoples of the world. Most of the historians of the nineteenth century attributed to the Indians every cruelty and evil that could be pictured by the pen of writer.

Theodore Roosevelt expresses an opinion of the Indian in the following passage from his sketch of the Algonquins in Part I of the "Winning of the West."

Not only were the Indians very terrible in battle, but they were cruel beyond all belief in victory; and the gloomy annals of border warfare are stained with their darkest hues because it was a war in which helpless women and children suffered the same hideous fate that so often befell their husbands and fathers. It was a war waged by savages against armed settlers, whose families followed them into the wilderness. Such a war is inevitably bloody and cruel; but the inhuman love of cruelty for cruelty's sake, which marked the red Indian above all other savages, rendered these wars more terrible than any others. For the hideous, unnamable, unthinkable tortures practiced by the red men on their captured foes, tender women and helpless children, were such as we read of in no other struggle.

While these outrages were doubtlessly committed in some instances cruelty was not innate with them. This is evidenced by the friendship of the Cherokees to the Oglethorpe settlements in Georgia, by Powhatan's fair treatment of the colonists at Jamestown and by the friendly relations which existed between the Pennsylvania Quakers and their copper colored neighbors. The bad traits of the Indians were developed and encouraged by the white man. The French, English and Spanish encroached on their hereditary lands from every direction and wherever possible used the native tribes as allies against one another. In the struggle for possession of territory claimed by these three rivals they encouraged and bribed the Indians to commit every atrocity with which they have been charged. These three representative Christian nations also frequently practiced the severest cruelties on their own prisoners, setting the example for the uncivilized savages. The Indians readily responded to fair and honorable treatment. Numerous instances of splendid spiritual natures are evidenced by such characters as Pocahontas, Nancy Ward, Atta-Kula-Kula, Logan, Sequoya and many others. In the early days there were many intermarriages between the white pioneers and the dusky forest maidens. From these marriages have come some of our most prominent statesmen and business men. A descendant of Princess Matoka (Pocahontas) has presided over the White House, while another descendant was the chief executive for the state of Virginia.

George Catlin, a lawyer and portrait painter, traveled from 1832 to 1839 among the wildest tribes of North American Indians and left a valuable contribution to Indian history both in his paintings and writings. He says:

I have roamed about from time to time during seven or eight years, visiting and associating with some three or four hundred thousand of these people, under an almost infinite variety of circumstance; and from the very many and decided voluntary acts of their hospitality and kindness I feel bound to pronounce them by nature a kind and hospitable people. The North American Indian in his native state is an honest, faithful, brave, war-like, cruel, revengeful, relentless, yet honorable, contemplative and religious being.

Bishop H. B. Whipple of Minnesota, in the preface to "A Century of Dishonor," writes only four years after the Custer Massacre:

The North American Indian is the noblest type of a heathen man on earth. He recognizes a Great Spirit; he believes in immortality; he has a quick intellect; he is a clear thinker; he is brave, and fearless and, until betrayed, he is true to his plighted faith; he has a passionate love for his children, and counts it joy to die for his people. Our most terrible wars have been with the noblest types of the Indians, and with men who had been the white man's friend.

Gene Stratton Porter in "A Word About the Bible" (McCall's Magazine, May, 1925) says, "I like to include the unwritten Bible of the North American Indians because they transmit as beautiful a conception of God, of duty and immortality as any religion in the world."

The Cherokees and other tribes received the Indian Territory as a compensation and atonement for one of the darkest crimes ever committed by a Christian nation.

Numerous other authorities can be produced to prove that the American Indian has probably been as much misjudged and as badly treated as any race of people that ever existed.

SKETCH TWO

The Scotch-Irish

The Scotch-Irish

EVER since the Stone Age, when the cave men hazarded forth with nothing but a heavy club for a weapon, there have been brave adventurers who were at all times ready to embark in quest of fame, fortune or new countries to explore. In this class may be placed the names of Columbus, Cortez, De Soto, Cabot, Hudson, Sir Walter Raleigh, Daniel Boone, George Rogers Clark and others.

There is, however, another kind of adventurer influenced by entirely different motives. This type has endured untold hardships and privations for the sake of an ideal without any hope or desire for renown. They have penetrated to the utmost parts of the earth and have left the impress of their characters wherever they have located, their sole quest being to find a land and found a home where they might enjoy civil and religious liberty.

The Scotch-Irish who first settled the

Holston Valleys were typical of this class, and to their bravery and hardihood is largely due the credit of settling the vast territory west of the Blue Ridge. As pioneers their courage was dauntless, their spirit unconquerable—they subdued the wilderness—conquered the red men and rendered valiant service to the cause of independence.

Joseph A. Waddell in his history of Augusta County says:

The history of the Scotch-Irish is necessarily a history of the troubles they suffered on account of their religion. It must be borne in mind however, that the great principle of religious liberty was not recognized in the seventeenth and the early part of the eighteenth centuries. The opinion prevailed that it was the duty of the civil government to maintain the church. In nearly all European countries some one church was established by law, and non-conformity to it was regarded as disloyal and punishable.

As a result of Tyrone's Rebellion in the reign of James I the North of Ireland was almost depopulated. Some 500,000 acres were confiscated by the crown and thrown open to settlement. Due to religious persecutions at home and to the fact that the new country promised an easier living, many of the Scotch Highlanders from the vicinity of

Aberdeen and Inverness quickly took advantage of the opportunity thus offered. From the year 1609 there was also a great emigration of Scotch Lowlanders to the province of Ulster.

Froude, speaking of the Scotch settlers in Ulster, says:

They went over to earn a living by labor, in a land which had produced hitherto trades and manufactures; they enclosed fields, raised farmhouses and homesteads where till then had been but robbers. They were saved from degenerating into the native type by their religion, then growing in its first enthusiasm into a living power which pervaded their entire being.

To trace the Scotch-Irish and ascertain whence came their ideals and patriotism it is necessary to go back twenty centuries. Off the west coast of Scotland, in a cold and inhospitable latitude, is located the little island of Iona. Its area comprises only about five square miles and it was inhabited by the Celts and Picts. Despite its isolation and ruggedness this little island is probably more responsible for the perpetuation and propagation of the Protestant religion than any other country. For many years it was the burial place of the Scottish kings, the reason for its selection being that it was the very source and center of the religion of their ancestors. It was from Iona that Scotland received the gospel, through the missionary work of the early Culdee church. Tertullian, the great Christian writer of the second century, was born about sixty years after the death of the Apostle John, who was the last of the Apostles. Tertullian says in his writings:

> These parts of Briton (northern Scotland) that were inaccessible to the Romans have become subject to Christ.

Spottiswood, the Scottish historian, writes:

> I verily think that under Domitian's persecutions some of the Apostle John's disciples first preached the Gospel in this kingdom.

Buchanan in his "History of Scotland" says:

> The Scotch were taught Christianity by the disciples of the Apostle John and many Christians of Britain, fearing the cruelty of Domitian, took the journey to Scotland, of whom many famous both in learning and integrity of life, stayed and fixed their habitations therein.

From such authentic and historical testimony we are justified in believing that

Christianity was introduced into Scotland early after the apostolic era and that it was of the purest type and free from materialism and civil alliances which caused so much trouble in the succeeding years. Columba established a missionary college on the island of Iona in the sixth century. This college sent out missionaries to all parts of Scotland who penetrated to the highland fastness and converted the inhabitants to Christianity. While the first emigrants from the highlands of Scotland to the province of Ulster in the North of Ireland were not noted for their piety they made rapid material progress. In 1625 a great religious revival swept over the province under the leadership of Josiah Walsh, a grandson of John Knox. From the date of this revival the religious character of the Scotch-Irish begins to influence their political and civil life. At this time Ireland was a dependency of England and the jurisdiction of the Established Church was extended over the former country. It is to the credit of James I that during his reign there was no distinction between the treatment of Conformists and Nonconformists.

During the reign of Charles I Archbishop Laud came into power and in 1632 he cited for trial certain prominent Scotch ministers, alleging that they were "fanatical disturbers of the peace of the Diocese." All four of the accused were deposed from the ministry and prohibited from preaching. Except for one or two short respites and during the interregnum under Cromwell there ensued a period of fifty years of persecution of the Scotch-Irish Presbyterian Church. During the existence of the commonwealth, however, the Presbyterians were not persecuted by the government.

Reid in his history of the Presbyterian Church in Ireland states:

At this time they were joined by many of the Episcopal clergy and from this period may be dated the commencement of the second Reformation.

The Episcopal Church being Calvinistic in its doctrine, it was but natural that these two principal exponents of Protestantism should be drawn closer together in the hour of trial and should amalgamate, in the defense of their ecclesiastic rights. Despite civil war in Ireland, and constant persecutions, by the year 1660 there were nearly one hundred congregations and a population of 100,000 adherents to the Calvinistic faith in the northern provinces.

For many years the Dissenters were harassed on account of marriages performed by their ministers. In the Bishops' court the marriages were declared to be void, the parties guilty of the sin of fornication, and their children pronounced illegitimate. James II came to the throne in 1685 and followed the example of King Rehoboam, who said to his people:

And now whereas my father did lade you with a heavy yoke, I will add to your yoke: my father chastised you with whips but I will chastise you with scorpions.

The Roman Catholics, being in high favor with King James, the Presbyterians made common cause with the Episcopalians in opposition to his intolerance and despotism. The Scotch-Irish were the first to espouse the cause of William of Orange, while the native Irish espoused the cause of King James.

In 1688 the Earl of Antrim laid siege to the town of Londonderry, which was the principal center of the Scotch-Irish. As

James' army advanced the entire rural population fled to the city for protection. Huddled in the confines of the gates were thousands of women and children whose only defense was the indomitable courage of their men folk. The city was unfortified, the garrison untrained in military defense and poorly armed, while the supply of provisions was entirely inadequate. Despite these handicaps the valiant defenders sustained the siege for three months. At the point of starvation, their ranks decimated by sickness, the brave garrison held out until help arrived. King James' army lost nearly ten thousand men during the various attacks. History scarcely reveals a parallel to the valor with which this siege was repelled.

Although England and Ireland were now safely Protestant under the wise rule of King William, Parliamentary relief for the Dissenters could not be obtained and the public exercise of their religion could not be observed, under heavy legal penalties William's efforts to obtain equal ecclesiastical rights and toleration for his dissenting subjects were frustrated by the High Church party. The matter of marriages by a Presbyterian minister was protested by the Irish bishops and they were held to be illegal, with the consequent civil and social stigma. Such conditions could not continue and the friction between the Presbyterians and the Established Church continued from one reign to the next.

Queen Anne succeeded William and placed herself under the guidance of the High Church Tories. In 1704 the Sacramental Test Act was passed excluding all Nonconformists from holding public office. In 1714 the Schism Bill was passed, which further prohibited them from teaching school. This was the final straw and from that time until 1774 a steady stream of Scotch-Irish emigrants poured into America. Entire congregations led by their pastor sailed on the same ship, bound for the same port. Most of the emigrants from the province of Ulster crossed to the mouth of Delaware Bay and landed in the vicinity of Philadelphia. This fertile section and temperate climate would seem to have been the Ultima Thule of their ambitions.

Waddell in his "Annals of Augusta County" says:

In 1729, near 6,000 Irish, nearly all Presbyterians, came to America, landing at Philadelphia. Before the middle of the century nearly 12,000 arrived annually for several years.

An unfavorable harvest in Ireland in 1739 further stimulated emigration and many of the very best citizens of Ulster joined the ever increasing tide. Among the passengers we find the names of many that are still familiar in the Holston Valleys. At this time came the Campbells, Breckenridges, Poages, Bells, Browns, Logans, Cummings, Kincannons, Blairs, Lairds, Cunninghams, Rheas, Shelbys, Kings, Prestons, Lewises and a host of others. They came first to Pennsylvania, because they thought the peace-loving Quakers would receive them with open arms. But alack and alas, the Quakers turned the cold shoulder on all the new arrivals and manifested special dislike for the Presbyterians, despite the fact that they themselves had but recently been driven out of England by religious intolerance.

Restrictive legislation having been passed against the Presbyterians, they determined to seek homes in Virginia, west of the Blue Ridge Mountains, "far from the madding crowd's ignoble strife." Once more the migration begins, this time overland in a southwesterly direction. Reid, in his history of the Presbyterian Church in Ireland, remarks that "the condition of the Presbyterians in Ireland must have been exceedingly unfavorable, if they could calculate on bettering their temporal condition in the wilds of America." Material gain was the least motive that influenced them; they were actuated by a desire for spiritual self-expression that would not be denied.

Governor Alexander Spotswood and his band of Cavaliers crossed the Blue Ridge Mountains and entered the Shenandoah Valley in 1716. So far as is known these were the first white men to enter the valley. Spotswood took possession of the valley in the name of the King of England and so impressed was he with the beauty of the mountains that he presented each member of his party with a golden horseshoe set with precious stones and founded the order of "Knights of the Golden Horseshoe."

John Lewis and his sturdy family had been forced by oppression to leave the province of Ulster and had settled with others of their copatriots in Lancaster County, Pennsylvania. Here again feeling the spirit of religious intolerance in the atmosphere, he and a small band of hardy Highlanders explored the lower Shenandoah Valley and settled in what is now Augusta County, Virginia, in the summer of 1732. Thus we have the trail broken for the countless hordes that were to follow.

Waddell draws a vivid picture of this emigration:

We may accompany, in imagination, these immigrants on their way from the settlements north of the Potomac, through the wilderness, to their future home. There was, of course, no road, and for the first comers no path to guide their steps, except, perhaps, the trail of the Indian or buffalo. They came at a venture, climbing the hills, fording the creeks and rivers and groping through the forests. At night they rested on the ground, with no roof over them but the broad expanse of heaven. After selecting a spot for a night's bivouac, and tethering their horses, fire was kindled by means of flint and steel, and their frugal meal was prepared. Only a scanty supply of food was brought along, for, as game abounded, they mainly "subsisted off the country." Before lying down to rest, many of them did not omit to worship the God of their fathers, and invoke His guidance and protection. The moon and stars looked down peacefully as they slumbered, while bears, wolves and panthers prowled around. It was impossible to bring wagons,

and all their effects were transported on horseback.
The list of articles was meagre enough. Clothing,
some bedding, guns and ammunition, a few cooking
utensils, seed corn, axes, saws, etc., and the Bible,
were indispensable, and were transported at whatever
cost of time and labor. Houses and furniture had to
be provided after the place of settlement was fixed
upon. The settlers were almost exclusively of the
Scotch-Irish race, natives of the north of Ireland,
but of Scottish ancestry. Most of those who came
during the first three or four decades were Dissenters
from the Church of England, of the Presbyterian
faith, and victims of religious persecution in their
native land. They were generally a profoundly religious people, bringing the Bible with them, whatever they had to leave behind, and as soon as possible
erected log meeting houses in which to assemble for
the worship of God, with school-houses hard by.

Search the human race and you cannot
find purer Anglo-Saxon stock than the descendants of the Scotch-Irish who settled in
the Appalachian Highlands. They were the
true pioneer stock, brave, inured to hardship
and dangers, of magnificent physique; nothing could withstand them. In the words of
Cæsar, they came, they saw and they conquered. There was another motive that
actuated the Scotch-Irish to penetrate the
unexplored valleys of the Shenandoah and
cause them to press onward to the valleys

of the Holston. Strong men have ever loved
the mountains, the Scotch-Irish were mostly
descendants of the Highlanders and they
thrived in the high altitudes. Possessed of a
deep religious fervor, their every act was
influenced by Holy Writ. Like King David
they believed that "Jehovah was the keeper
of His people" and they felt that He was
nearer in the mountains than on the plains.

> I will lift up mine eyes unto the mountains:
> From whence shall my help come?
> My help cometh from Jehovah
> Who made heaven and earth.
> He that keepeth thee will not slumber.
> Jehovah will keep thy going out and thy coming in
> From this time forth and forevermore.

This was their faith and they walked in it.
No expedition of any consequence was undertaken unless accompanied by the pastor
of the congregation. Thus we find many of
the early pastors were militant preachers,
bearing arms and often in the forefront of
battle.

SKETCH THREE
The Trans-Alleghany Country

SKETCH THREE

The Trans-Alleghany Country

THE early Colonial charters of Virginia described her boundaries as including all of the territory lying between latitude 36° 30' and 42° extending from the Atlantic Ocean to the South Seas. Little was known of the geography of the new continent and little did the British sovereign dream that he was including in this grant the fourth of a continent. For one hundred years after the colonization of Virginia the settlements were confined to the Piedmont section east of the Appalachians. Very vague ideas existed as to the nature of the country west of the Blue Ridge Mountains. In fact many thought that the mountains were impassable, others that the Indian Ocean was just on the other side and still another theory was that the Great Lakes could easily be seen from the summit of the higher peaks. Consequently, the western boundaries of the counties were very vague indeed.

Previous to 1738 the county of Orange, Virginia, included all of the territory west of the mountains. In this year the counties of Frederick and Augusta were cut off from Orange County. All of the territory west of the Blue Ridge Mountains was included in the county of Augusta and her western boundaries extended to the Mississippi River.

This immense territory, included in one county, at the present time comprises four states: West Virginia, Kentucky, Tennessee and Ohio. Augusta County was not organized until 1745, there not being a sufficient number of magistrates to constitute a court.

Botetourt County was formed from Augusta in 1769 and its western boundaries were also supposed to be the Mississippi River. Fincastle County was cut off from Botetourt in 1772. The civil divisions still being entirely too large and many of the settlers remote from the county seats, the General Assembly of Virginia passed an act on December 6, 1776, providing that the county of Fincastle should be divided into three counties. These subdivisions were to be the counties of Montgomery, Washington and Kentucky. Washington County, Virginia, was the first place in the United States to be named for General George Washington.

At this time it was thought that a large portion of what is now Sullivan County, Tennessee, was in the state of Virginia. Virginia jurisdiction was extended and taxes collected as far as Fort Patrick Henry and Long Island. The boundary between the western portion of Virginia and the eastern part of Tennessee was not fully settled until the compromise line of 1802 was established. This line ran through what is now State Street, Bristol, and placed Long Island and the site of the present city of Kingsport in the state of Tennessee.

While there is strong evidence that the Holston Valley was visited by trappers and Indian traders early in the eighteenth century, the first organized expedition was not undertaken until 1748. In that year southwest Virginia and east Tennessee were explored by a party consisting of Dr. Thomas Walker, Col. James Patton, Col. John Buchanan, Col. James Woods and Maj. Charles Campbell. They found Samuel

Stalnaker already established on the headwaters of the Holston River, in what is now
the upper end of Washington County. He
is the first known settler to make a home in
this section. Dr. Thomas Walker and Col.
James Patton were representatives of the
Loyal Company of London, and were also
interested as shareholders. This Company
had grants from the King of England for
800,000 acres, west of the Blue Ridge Mountains. Dr. Thomas Walker surveyed and
entered large tracts of land for his company.
In 1749 Dr. Walker visited Long Island and
in that year surveyed and entered 224 tracts
containing 45,249 acres in southwest Virginia, Tennessee and Kentucky.

The first recorded survey of land in Sullivan
County was for Edmund Pendleton and was
made April 2, 1750. It was for 3,000 acres
on West Creek, a branch of Indian River.
This track was at the foot of Eden's
Ridge a few miles from Kingsport. The
English government at first encouraged
settlements west of the Blue Ridge for two
reasons. This section offered a convenient
home for the Dissenters from the Church of
England and the colonization of this terri-

tory served to check the advance of the French from the north and west. The French had infiltrated the Mississippi Valley from Canada and it was their avowed purpose to confine the English settlements to east of the mountains.

June 14, 1749, the grant to the Loyal Company was renewed and the time extended for making surveys. At this time the price of land was three pounds per hundred acres. This cheap land appealed to the thrifty Scotch and they flocked down the valley of Virginia in considerable numbers. During the ten years from 1760 until 1770 settlements had been made on New River, at Fort Chiswell, Black's Fort (now Abingdon), Shelby's Fort (now Bristol), Long Island (now Kingsport) and other points in Sullivan and Washington counties, Tennessee.

In studying the people of the Holston Valleys it must be borne in mind that they were an entirely different people from those who settled tidewater Virginia. While most of the pioneers to the Holston Valleys were Scotch-Irish, there was an admixture of English, German, Irish, and French Huguenots. However, it only required a very short

time to amalgamate them into one people—
they were Americans first. They had cut
loose from the Old World and its traditions
and they were now in the full enjoyment of
civil rights and religious freedom. Strong
proof of this is shown by the fact that the
Scotch-Irish were the first to draw up a
declaration of their rights to religious
freedom and representative government.

When Frye and Jefferson surveyed the line
between Virginia and North Carolina in
1749 they abruptly terminated their work
at a place called Steep Rock in Johnson
County, Tennessee. The end of this line was
never located and the controversy over the
location was not settled until a hundred
years later when the Supreme Court of the
United States held that the compromise line
of 1802 was the correct line.

Sullivan County was erected in 1779. "The
original boundary of the county began at
Steep Rock; thence along the dividing ridge
that separates the waters of the Great
Kanawha and Tennessee, to the head of
Indian Creek; thence along the ridge that
divides the waters of the Holston and
Watauga; thence direct to the highest point

of Chimney Top Mountain, at the Indian boundary.''

The official organization of Sullivan County took place at the house of Moses Looney, February 7, 1780. The justices of the peace present were Isaac Shelby, David Looney, Gilbert Christian, John Duncan, William Wallace, Samuel Smith, Henry Clark, Anthony Bledsoe, George Maxwell, John Anderson and Joseph Martin.

John Rhea was appointed clerk and Nathan Clark sheriff. Isaac Shelby exhibited a commission from Governor Caswell of North Carolina, dated November 19, 1779, appointing him Colonel-Commandant of the county. Other commissions appointed Henry Clark Lieutenant-Colonel, David Looney first Major and John Shelby second Major.

William Cocke was admitted to practice law in February, 1782, the first lawyer we have any record of in Sullivan County.

For six years, the county seat was in the neighborhood of Eaton's Station, or what we now call Eden's Ridge, about four miles from the present city of Kingsport.

When Hawkins County was erected in 1786 it was found necessary to build a courthouse at a more central location in the county, and a commission composed of Joseph Martin, James McNeil, John Duncan, Evan Shelby, Samuel Smith, William King and John Scott were named to select a site for the courthouse.

Up to 1792, this commission had not reported, but in that year a tract of thirty acres on the present site of Blountville was conveyed to John Anderson, George Maxwell and Richard Gammon whereon the county buildings were to be erected. It took another set of commissioners, however, before the work was completed, and in 1795 the following appear to have been selected: George Rutledge, James Gaines, John Shelby, Jr., John Anderson, Jr., David Terry and Joseph Wallace.

The first courthouse was built of logs and was, of its kind, a massive structure. It was built on the south side of Main Street nearly opposite the present courthouse. The jail was placed in the rear.

It was in the same year, 1795, that Blountville became the county seat. About thirty years after the first courthouse was built in the town a brick one replaced it, which served until 1853, when another more pretentious brick one was erected. The building, with its contents, was destroyed by fire during the battle in September, 1863; the walls remained intact, however, and the building was rebuilt. A modern building was erected in 1920 on the same site as the previous one. Three jails have been built to accompany the courthouse—the first immediately in the rear of the building, the second on a lot adjoining, also in the rear, and the third between the sites of the first and the second.

The Sullivan County records, with the exception of the deed books, for eighty years, from 1780 to 1860, were destroyed during the war between the states. The land records were carried out of the courthouse by Frederick Sturm, Register, and all were saved. Much valuable history was lost through the destruction of the court records.

SKETCH FOUR
The Beginning of Kingsport

SKETCH FOUR

The Beginning of Kingsport

King's Mill Station was at the mouth of Reedy Creek, near the present site of Kingsport, Sullivan County, Tennessee, in the year 1774. "Dunmore's War," page 252.

JAMES KING, after whom Kingsport was named, the first of the name to seek his fortune in America, was born in London in 1752. He first settled in Montgomery County, Virginia, but was attracted by accounts of the beautiful and fertile valleys of the Holston. He moved to Sullivan County, Tennessee, probably prior to 1774, and built a mill at the mouth of Reedy Creek, which was known as King's Mill. He served in the Point Pleasant campaign in Captain Pauling's company of Botetourt troops. He also served in a number of battles during the Revolutionary War and was wounded at Guilford Courthouse. He recovered from his wound and was present at the surrender of Cornwallis at Yorktown. He was an ardent patriot, a man of considerable initiative and rendered valiant service to the Colonies. In 1784 he built an iron furnace at the mouth of Steele's Creek in Sullivan County. This was the first iron furnace erected in the state of Tennessee.

Dr. Thomas Walker conducted the first organized expedition into the Holston Valley in 1748 with a party of surveyors. His second expedition was principally for purposes of exploration. Leaving his home east of the Blue Ridge Mountains, March 6, 1750, he reached the junction of the north and south forks of the Holston on March 31, having followed down Reedy Creek. The following account is taken from his diary, which fortunately was preserved:

March 31st. We kept down Reedy Creek to Holston where we measured an Elm 25 feet round 3 feet from the ground. We saw young Sheldrakes, we went down the River to the North Fork and up the North Fork about a quarter of a mile to a Ford and then crossed it. In the Fork between Holston's and the North River, are five Indian Houses built with logs and covered with bark, and there were abundance of Bones, some whole Pots and Pans, some broken and many pieces of mats and Cloth. On the West Side of the North River is four Indian Houses such as before mentioned, we went four miles Below the North River

RUINS OF THE OLD KING'S MILL STATION TAVERN, OLD KINGSPORT

and Camped on the Banks of Holston's, opposite to a
large Indian Fort.

April ye 1st. The Sabath. We saw Perch, Mullets,
and Carp in plenty, and caught one of the large Sort
of Cat Fish. I marked my Name, the day of the
Month, and date of the year on several Beech Trees.

2nd. We left Holston & travelled through small
Hills till about Noon, when one of our Horses being
choaked by eating Reeds too greedily, we stopped,
having travelled seven miles.

Dr. Walker continued his journey through
Cumberland Gap into Kentucky, where he
explored a considerable portion of the eastern part of this state.

In July of this year, 1757, Richard Pearis, who was
located on the Holston River carrying on a trade with
the Cherokee Indians, addressed a letter to the Governor of Virginia requesting a grant for the lands on the
Long Island in the South Fork of the Holston River.
In reply the Governor encouraged Pearis to believe
that he could obtain a grant, and wrote him as
follows: "I am surprised the inhabitants on Holston
river should submit to be robbed by a few Indians.
Let the Chickasaw know that I greatly approve of
his conduct and have a real esteem for him." This
last sentence in the Governor's letter had reference
to a Chickasaw warrior who had resented the murder
of one of the white settlers.—Summer's "History of
Southwest Virginia."

In 1756, Governor Dinwiddie, in order to
enlist the Cherokees as allies against the

French, directed Major Andrew Lewis to
enlist a force of sixty men and construct a
fort in the Cherokee country on the Tennessee River.

Major Lewis collected his forces and
started on this expedition in June. His route
followed the Holston River, past Long
Island, to the Tennessee River about thirty
miles below the present site of Knoxville.
The fort was built and was garrisoned by
two hundred British soldiers. It was named
Fort Loudon. In 1760 some bands of Cherokees, returning through southwest Virginia
from their campaign against the French,
took some horses from the settlers to replace
those they had lost in their northern journey.
They were attacked by the Virginians and a
number of their party killed. This incident
quickly turned the Cherokee allies into
deadly enemies, and the war cry was sent
ringing along the borders. The Fort Loudon
garrison was attacked and the fort besieged.
The Governor of Virginia directed Colonel
William Byrd to raise a body of six hundred
men and rush to the relief of the fort. Colonel
Byrd and his forces made very slow progress
as they spent most of the time in building

JAMES KING
FOUNDER OF KING'S MILL STATION

roads and blockhouses. They proceeded to
the lead mines in Wythe County for a supply
of lead and built a fort about eight miles
west of Wytheville, Virginia, on the present
Lee Highway. The fort was named Fort
Chiswell, after Colonel John Chiswell.
Colonel Byrd then proceeded to open a road to
Long Island at the forks of the Holston River.

At this point, Col. Byrd and his men spent the
winter of 1760. During the winter Col. Byrd erected
a fort upon a beautiful level on the north bank of the
South Fork of the Holston river, nearly opposite the
upper end of Long Island, to which fort he gave the
name of Fort Robinson, in honor of John Robinson,
the partner of himself and Col. John Chiswell in the
ownership of the lead mines. This fort was built
upon an extensive plan. The walls were sufficient in
thickness to withstand the force of a small cannon
shot. There were proper bastions, and the gates were
spiked with large nails so that the wood was entirely
covered.

After a siege lasting for some time the
garrison at Fort Loudon was compelled to
surrender to the Cherokees. Only a remnant
of the defenders escaped death by starvation
or at the hands of the red men, and finally
succeeded in joining the expedition which
had been sent to their relief.

Fort Loudon was defended by twelve great

guns. It cannot be explained how these cannon had been transported to Fort Loudon as early as 1756. They could not have been brought down the Ohio and up the Tennessee, for the French were in possession of the mouth of the Tennessee. The only plausible explanation that can be given is that these cannon were carried across the mountains from Augusta County when reinforcements were sent to Fort Loudon, and thence along Indian trails on sleds or runners. It is probable that they were brought from Fort Lewis near Salem, Virginia, to the waters of the Holston, at Long Island, and carried down the same in boats or canoes to the mouth of the Holston, and thence via the Tennessee to Fort Loudon.

In the winter of 1768–69 a great flood of settlers poured into southwestern Virginia and as far as Boone's Creek in Tennessee.

Gilbert Christian and William Anderson were with Colonel Byrd's expedition of 1760 and had visited Long Island. They returned in 1769 to explore the country and penetrated as far as Big Creek in Hawkins County. Here they encountered a large force of Indians and returned.

Christian's Campaign into Cherokee Country

Christian's Campaign into Cherokee Country

O N the first day of August, 1776, the Virginia Council of Defense ordered that a commission be issued to Colonel William Christian and that he be commander-in-chief of two battalions of troops that were to proceed at once in an offensive against the southern Indians. The following captains, with their companies, accompanied this expedition. As practically all of them took active part in future Indian wars, as well as the war for independence, their names are entitled to be preserved in the history of this section.

Captain JOHN CAMPBELL
Captain WILLIAM RUSSELL
Captain HOBERT BOGGS
Captain JOHN SEVIER
Captain JAMES THOMPSON
Captain ISAAC BLEDSOE
Captain JOHN MONTGOMERY
Captain DANIEL SMITH

Captain AARON LEWIS
Captain JACOB WOMACK
Captain WILLIAM COCKE
Captain BENJAMIN GRAY
Captain WILLIAM PRESTON
Captain THOMAS MADISON

Rev. Charles Cummings and Rev. Joseph Rhea accompanied the first battalion as chaplains. Colonel William Christian, with his command proceeded to Long Island on the Holston (Kingsport). Here they were joined by troops from North Carolina under Major Winston. On the first day of August, 1776, the Virginia Council gave the following instructions to Colonel William Christian as commander-in-chief of all the forces.

When your battalion and the battalion under Colonel Charles Lewis are completed, you are to march with them and the forces under the command of Colonel Russell, and such others as may join you from Carolina, into the Cherokee country, if these forces shall be judged sufficient for the purpose of severly chastising that cruel and perfidious nation, which you are to do in a manner most likely to put a stop to future insults and ravages and that may redound most the honor of American arms. If the Indians should be reduced to the necessity of suing for peace, you must take care to demand of them a sufficient number of their chiefs and warriors as hostages, for the performance of the conditions you may require of them. You must insist on their delivering up all prisoners who may choose to leave them and on their giving up to justice all persons amongst them who have been concerned in bringing on the present war, particularly Stuart, Cameron and Gist, and all others who have committed murder or robberies on our frontiers. You may require any other terms which the situation of affairs may point out and you may judge necessary for the safety and honor of the Commonwealth. You must endeavor to communicate with the commanding officer of the Carolina forces and cooperate with him, making the attack as near the time of his as may be.

You are from time to time to write His Excellency the Governor, giving him a full account of your operations, and requiring his further instructions.

Instructions to Colonel Charles Lewis of the second battalions of minute men: You are to order the captains under your command to march their companies to their respective counties, then to discharge such of their men as are not properly qualified to serve on an expedition against the Indians. and to raise with all possible dispatch in their stead the best recruits that can be found for the service, and, having so completed their companies, to repair to the Big Island on Holston river in Fincastle county, the place of general rendezvous.

In the month of September, 1776, that portion of the troops under the command of Colonel William Russell began their march to the Great Island of the Holston, at which time Anthony Bledsoe entered two wagons in the public service, to convey the baggage and provision of the troops. This circumstance is mentioned, for the reason that this was the first time, as far as can be ascertained, that a wagon was taken by the white man as far down as Long Island in the Holston (Kingsport, Tenn.).

By the first of October Colonel Christian had mobilized at Long Island (now Kingsport) a force of 2,000 men, each soldier was supplied with one pound of powder and fifty bullets. Only one company, under the command of Colonel John Sevier, was mounted, the rest of the army being infantry. The forces having all reported to Colonel Christian at Long Island, a start was made for the enemy's country early in October. The first night they camped at the foot of Chimney Top Mountain, which towers over the surrounding ranges southwest of Kingsport. Colonel Christian was familiar with Indian warfare and advanced with the utmost caution. Spies were kept continually ahead of his forces to prevent the possibility of an ambuscade. The Indian chieftains had repeatedly boasted that the white man's army should never cross the French Broad River.

Junction of North and South Forks of Holston River at Rotherwood

Consequently a stiff resistance was expected at this point. For some unknown reason, or because they were dismayed at the formidable array made by Christian's army, no resistance was offered at the crossing of the French Broad.

Colonel Christian pressed on into the enemy's country and destroyed a number of their towns and crops but met with no opposition as the entire Cherokee nation had fled to the mountain fastnesses. The Indian town of Echotas was not burned from the fact that it was the home of Nancy Ward, who had befriended the whites in so many ways. In November the Cherokees sued for peace, and a truce was agreed upon, which was to be followed by a treaty to be made at Long Island during 1777. The Indians having been severely punished and their spirit broken, Colonel Christian withdrew his command from the Indian country and returned to Long Island. Fort Robinson having been rebuilt and rechristened Fort Patrick Henry, Colonel Christian left a garrison of six hundred men in command of Evan Shelby and Anthony Bledsoe and disbanded the remainder of his army.

THE TREATY OF LONG ISLAND

July 2, 1777, was a momentous day in the history of Long Island and the Holston settlements.

In accordance with the truce agreed upon the previous year the mighty chiefs of the Cherokee nation with their retainers and braves had gathered at this historic spot. Among those present were Oconosta of Chota, Rayetach of Toquoe, the Raven of Chota, Oo-tosse-eteh of Hiwassee, Ooskuah of Chilhowie, Atta-Kula-Kula of Natchey Creek, the Terrapin of Chilestooch, Sunne Wauh of Big Island and many others. Also came Colonel William Preston, Colonel William Christian and Colonel Evan Shelby, commissioners for Virginia duly appointed by His Excellency Governor Patrick Henry. North Carolina was represented by Waighstill Avery, William Sharpe, Robert Lanier and Joseph Coniston. The Fourth of July was duly observed, being the first anniversary of the Declaration of Independence. As was the custom when treating with the Indians there were many ''Big Talks'' and much ceremony observed.

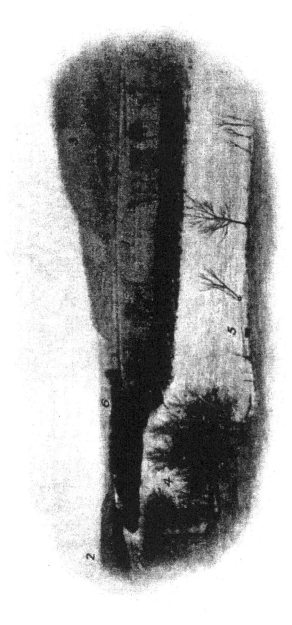

HISTORIC LONG ISLAND

1. The Island
2. Island Flats and Fort
   Patrick Henry (beyond the ridge)
3. Bay's Mountain

4. Tilthammer Shoals
5. Tilthammer Rock
6. Indian War Path
7. Sluice of Holston River

This treaty was soon broken by the white men, who persisted in encroaching on the Indian territory. The distant lands always seemed more attractive to the settler and he pushed over the Indian boundaries, in his quest for fertile land, with no thought for the consequences of his act.

After many days of parleying a treaty was finally agreed upon on July 20, 1776. The Cherokees were forced out of their rightful heritage whose boundaries originally comprised an empire embracing the richest natural resources to be found on the American continent.

The boundaries agreed upon between the commissioners and the Cherokee chiefs were as follows:

That the boundary line between the State of North Carolina and the said Over-Hill Cherokees shall forever hereafter be and remain as follows, (to wit) Beginning at a point in the dividing line which during the treaty hath been agreed upon between the said Over-Hill Cherokees and the State of Virginia, where the line between that state and North Carolina (hereafter to be extended) shall cross or intersect the same, running thence a right line to the north bank of the Holston River at the mouth of Cloud's Creek, being the second creek below the Warrior's Ford, at the mouth of Carter's Valley, thence a right line to the highest point of a mountain called the High Rock or Chimney Top, from thence a right line to the mouth of Camp Creek, otherwise called McNama's Creek, on the south bank of Nolichucky River, about ten miles or thereabouts below the mouth of Great Limestone, be the same more or less, and from the mouth of Camp Creek aforesaid a south-east course into the mountains which divide the hunting grounds of the middle settlements from those of the Over-Hill Cherokees.

It was with the greatest reluctance that the Cherokees yielded Long Island. For generations it had been held sacred as their treaty ground. Many peace pacts had been held on this mystic island, many peace pipes had been smoked here and the council fire had burned many times.

So great was the sentiment attached to this strip of land that a protest memorandum was entered into the treaty as follows:

The Tassell yesterday objected to giving up Great Island, opposite to Fort Henry, to any person or country whatsoever, except Colonel Nathaniel Gist, for whom and themselves it was reserved by the Cherokees. The Raven did the same, this day, in behalf of his people and desired that Colonel Gist might sit down upon it when he pleased as it belonged to him and them to hold good talks on.

Petty border warfare continued and in 1779 Colonel Evan Shelby led a campaign against the Chickamaugas who resided near Lookout Mountain (Chattanooga) on the Tennessee River. Colonel Shelby collected his troops at Long Island (Kingsport). With nearly one thousand men at his command he adopted a different style of warfare. Boats were built for the entire command and they swiftly descended the Holston and Tennessee rivers to Chickamauga, the Indian stronghold. Dragging Canoe with five hundred warriors fled on the approach of Shelby's army and his town was destroyed. As the Indian chiefs did not respond to his request that they come in and make peace, Shelby destroyed twelve of their towns and vast stores of corn. Quantities of goods as well as horses were also captured and confiscated. After this chastisement Shelby destroyed his boats and returned overland to Long Island. His men had to march over two hundred miles through a trackless wilderness and suffered much on this return journey.

Dunmore's War

SKETCH SIX
Dunmore's War

FROM the beginning of the 18th century the Scotch-Irish and German settlers of Virginia and Pennsylvania kept pushing steadily westward. This involved constant encroachment on the Indian lands and many minor conflicts with them. Indian resentment blazed forth in 1763 in Pontiac's conspiracy, and was not subdued by Boquet's retaliatory expedition. The introduction of firearms and fire water into the Indian tribes did not improve the situation. The red men in almost every instance where they first came in contact with the whites showed a disposition to be friendly and share their lands with the settlers. The first pioneers, however, could not help but look with avaricious eyes upon the fertile valleys and wooded uplands that stretched westward to the setting sun. Imbued with the Anglo-Saxon idea of racial supremacy they continued encroaching on the hunting grounds of the Indians. Real peace was impossible under these conditions. The differences were irreconcilable; clashes and individual tragedies were inevitable. While precipitated by a set of tragedies which occurred on the upper Ohio, Dunmore's War was the culmination of a series of grievances and outrages, which were first perpetrated by the white man and retaliated by the red man.

Every effort was made to pacify the Indians by promises and peace treaties, but the treaties were invariably violated by the whites with the usual reprisals by the red men. Theodore Roosevelt made an exhaustive study of the circumstances which led to the Indian wars. In his "Winning of the West" he sets forth these conditions as he found them.

The history of the border wars, both in the ways they were begun and in the ways they were waged, makes a long tale of injuries inflicted, suffered, and mercilessly revenged. It could not be otherwise when brutal, reckless, and lawless borderers, despising all men not their own color, were thrown in contact with savages who esteemed cruelty and treachery as the highest virtues, and rapine and murder as the worthiest of pursuits. Moreover, it was sadly inevitable that the law-abiding borderer as well as the white ruffian, the peaceful Indian as well as the painted marauder, should be plunged into the struggle to suffer the punishment that should only have fallen on their evilminded fellows.

Looking back, it is easy to say that much of the wrong-doing could have been prevented, but if we examine the facts to find out the truth, not to establish a theory, we are bound to admit that the struggle was really one that could not possibly have been avoided.

Mere outrages could be atoned for or settled; the question which lay at the root of our difficulties was that of the occupation of the land itself, and to this there could be no solution save war. The Indians had no ownership of land in the way in which we understand the term. The tribes lived far apart; each had for its hunting grounds all the territory from which it was not barred by rivals. Each looked with jealousy upon all interlopers, but each was prompt to act as an interloper when occasion offered. Every good hunting ground was claimed by many nations. It was rare, indeed, that any tribe had an uncontested title to a large tract of land; where such titles existed, it rested not on actual occupancy and cultivation, but on the recent butchery of weaker rivals. For instance, there were a dozen tribes, all of whom hunted in Kentucky, and fought each other there, all of whom had equally good titles to the soil, and not one of whom acknowledged the right of any other, as a matter of fact they had therein no right, save the right of the strongest. The land no more belonged to them than it belonged to Boone and the white hunters who first visited it.

Throughout 1773 the dread of another

Indian invasion was the constant fear of the settlers in the Holston Valley. Subsequent events proved their fears were not groundless. During the month of September the family of John Roberts living on Reedy Creek near the present site of Kingsport were all either killed or captured by a party of Shawnees and Mingoes under the leadership of their famous chief John Logan.* In October, James Boone, eldest son of Daniel Boone, and Henry Russell, son of Captain William Russell, were waylaid and killed near Castlewood, in Russell County, Virginia; probably by the same party who killed the Roberts family.

*Logan was the perpetrator of this massacre which was really the cause of Dunmore's war. During the French and Indian War he remained neutral and took refuge in Philadelphia. For this he was compelled to leave his old home and, about 1772, settled in Ohio. Here in his town, on Yellow Creek, April 30, 1774, his people were massacred. Logan swore to have revenge—that he would never stop killing until he had satisfied his thirst for blood. He made four raids, sparing none who came within his grasp—men, women, and children he slew with savage cruelty. His acts brought on Dunmore's war culminating in the battle on the Great Kanawha. When the chiefs were summoned before Dunmore to discuss terms of peace, Logan failed to appear. Dunmore sent for him and received a reply, saying he was a warrior, not a maker of peace, and at the same time delivered what is conceded the most eloquent speech in savage history. It is familiar to most readers and runs as follows:

"I appeal to any white man to say if ever he entered Logan's cabin hungry and he gave him not meat; if ever he came cold and naked and he clothed him not? During the course of the last long and bloody war, Logan remained idle in his camp, an advocate of peace. Such was my love for the whites that my countrymen pointed as I passed and said, 'Logan is the friend of the white man.' I had even thought to have lived with you, but for the injuries of one man. Colonel Cresap, the last spring, in cold blood and unprovoked, murdered all the relations of Logan not even sparing my women and children. There runs not a drop of my blood in the veins of any living creature. This called on me for revenge. I have sought it. I have killed many. I have fully glutted my vengeance. For my country I rejoice at the beams of peace; but do not harbor a thought that mine is the joy of fear. Logan never felt fear. He will not turn on his heel to save his life. Who is there to mourn for Logan? Not one." ("Historic Sullivan")

The Indians very rarely went on the warpath in the winter, but the spring of 1774 found the Mingoes and Shawnees smouldering like a firebrand ready to burst into flame at the slightest disturbance. John Connolly was the personal representative of Lord Dunmore, governor of Virginia, on the northern frontier. Connolly was a hot-headed military man, lacking in diplomacy and discretion. He issued an open letter warning the settlers to arm themselves and be in a position to repel attack, as the Shawnees were hostile. This letter practically had the effect of a declaration of war.

A number of the relatives and friends of the great Indian chief Logan were plied with liquor and then brutally murdered on Yellow Creek, Pennsylvania, by a party of rough borderers led by a man named Greathouse. The Mingoes sent out runners and urged other tribes to join them in a war of extermination. They incited all of the adjacent tribes as far south as the Cherokees of Tennessee. By the end of April, 1774, the entire frontier was involved. Blazing cabins, tortured and scalped women, children and men told the story in unmistakable language.

Dunmore's War was on. Connolly had started something he could not stop. Here is where the brave pioneers of the Holston settlements won their claim to lasting renown. General Andrew Lewis was commissioned by Lord Dunmore to raise an army of 1,500 fighting men from west of the Blue Ridge. At this time the county of Fincastle extended from the Blue Ridge Mountains westward to the Mississippi River. The Fincastle men were from the valleys of the Holston, Clinch, Watauga and New River settlements, enlisted under the command of Colonel William Christian.

The recruits from southwestern Virginia and east Tennessee were enlisted under Captains Daniel Smith, William Campbell and Evan Shelby. Colonel Lewis was instructed to proceed to the flats of Greenbrier, or what is now Lewisburg, West Virginia, where he would be joined by Lord Dunmore and they would then proceed against the Indian towns in Ohio. Colonel Lewis brought his men safely through the wilderness to the junction of the Kanawha and Ohio rivers. Here they encamped awaiting the arrival of Lord Dunmore. They were attacked at sunrise on

ISAAC SHELBY

October 10, by a force of 1,200 Indians under command of their great Chief Cornstalk. An account of the battle is graphically given in a letter of Isaac Shelby to his uncle, John Shelby. This is probably a copy of the official account of the battle prepared by Colonel Andrew Lewis. (Original spelling preserved)

Camp Opposite to the Mouth of Great Canaway
October 16th, 1774.

Dear Uncle—

I gladly embrace this oppertunity to Acquaint You that we are all three yet alive th(r)o Gods Mercies & I Sincerely wish that this may find you & your family in the Station of Health that we left you. I never had any thing Worth Notice to quaint you with since I left you till now, the Express seems to be Hurrying that I Cant write you with the same Coolness & Deliberation as I would; we arrived at the mouth (of) Canaway Thursday 6th Octr. and incamped on a fine piece of Ground with an intent to wait for the Governor & his party but hearing that he was going another way we Contented our selves to stay there a few days to rest the troops &c when we looked upon our selves to be in safely till Monday morning the 10th Instant with two of our Compys. went out before day to hunt, To wit Valentine Sevier & Jas. Robison & Discovered a party of Indians; as I expect you will hear something of our Battle before you get this I have here stated this affair nearly to you.

OFFICIAL ACCOUNT OF THE BATTLE

For the Satisfaction of the people in your parts in this they have a true state of the Memorable Battle faught at the mouth of the great Canaway on the 10th Instant; Monday morning about half an Hour before sunrise two of Capt Russells Compy. discovered a large party of indians about a mile from Camp one of which men was killed the Other made his Escape & brought in his intilligence; in two or three minutes affter Colo. Andrew Lewis being informed thereof Immediately ordered Colo. Charles Lewis to take the Command of 150 men from Augusta and with him went Capt Dickison. Capt. Harrison, Capt. Willson, Capt. Jno. Lewis from Augusta and Capt. Lockridge which made the firest division Colo. Fleming was also ordered to take the Command of one hundred & fifty men Cŏnsisting of Botetourt Capt. Shelby & Capt Russell of Fincastle which made the second Division. Colo. Lewis marched with his Division to the Right some Distance up from the Ohio to the left; Colo. Lewis's Division had not marched Little more than a quarter of a mile from Camp; when about sunrise, an attack was made on the first Division in a most Vigirous manner by the United Tribes of Indians—Shawnees, Delawares, Mingoes, Taways, and of several Other Nations in Number not less than Eight Hundred and by many thaught to be a thousand; in this Heavy Attack Colonel Charles Lewis received a wound which soon after Caused his Death and several of his men fell in the spott in fact the Augusta Division was forced to give way to the heavy fire of the Enemy in about a second of a minute after the Attack on Colo. Lewiss Division the Enemy Engaged the Front of Colo. Flemings Division on the Ohio;

and in short time Colo. Fleming recd. two balls thro
his left Arm and one thro his breast; and after anni-
mating the Captains and souldiers in a Calm manner
to the pursuit of Victory returned to Camp, the loss
of the Brave Colonels was Sensibly felt by the Officers
in perticular, But the Augusta troops being shortly
Reinforced from Camp by Colonel Field with his Company together with Capt. McDowell, Capt. Mathews
& Capt. Stuart from Augusta, Capt. John Lewis,
Capt. Paulin, Capt. Arbuckle & Capt. McClanahan
from Botetourt, the Enemy no longer able to Maintain their Ground was forced to give way till they
were in a Ling with the troops left in action on
Bancks of Ohio, by Colo. Fleming in this precipitate
retreat Colo. Field was killed, after which Capt.
Shelby was ordered to take the Commd. During this
time which was till after twelve of the Clock, the
Action continued Estreemly Hott, the Close under-
wood many steep bancks, & Loggs greatly favored
their retreat, and the Bravest of their men made the
use of themselves, whilst others were throwing their
dead into the Ohio, and Carrying of(f) their wounded,
after twelve the Action in a small degree abated but
Continued sharp Enough till after one oClock. Their
long retreat gave them a most advantageous spot of
ground; from whence it Appeared to the Officers so
difficult to dislodge them that it was thought most
adviseable to stand at the line then was formed which
was about a mile and a quarter in length, and had
till then sustained a Constand and Equal weight of
fire from wing to wing, it was till half an Hour of
Sun sett they Continued firing on us which we returned to their Disadvantage at length Night Coming
on they found a safe retreat They had not the satisfac-

tion of scalping any of our men save One or two
stragles whom they Killed before the engagement
many of their dead they scalped rather than we
should have them but our troops scalped Twenty of
those who were first killed; Its beyond a Doubt their
loss in November far Exceeds ours, which is Considerable.

Field Officers Killed Colo. Charles Lewis, and Colo.
Jno. Fields, Field Officers wounded Colo. Willm
Fleming; Capts. Killed John Murray, Capt Saml.
Willson, Capt. Robt. McClanahan, Capt. Jas. Ward,
Captains wounded Thos. Buford, John Dickinson &
John Scidmore, Subbalterns Killed Lieutenant Hugh
Allen, Ensign Mathew Brakin, Ensign Cundiff, Sub-
balterns wounded, Lieut. Lard, Lieut. Bance, Lieut.
Goldman, Lieut Jas. Robinson about 46 killed &
about 80 wounded from this Sir you may Judge that
we had a Very hard day its realy Impossible for me
to Express or you to Conceive Acclamations that we
were under, sometimes, the Hidious Cries of the
Enemy and the groans of our wounded men Lying
around was Enough to shuder the stoutest hart its
the general Opinion of the Officers that we shall
soon have another Ingagement as we have now got
Over into the Enemys Country; we expect to meet the
Governor about forty or fifty miles from here nothing
will save us from another Battle Unless they Attack
the Governors Party, five men that came in Dadys
(daddy's) Company were killed, I dont know that
you were Acquainted with any of them Except Marck
Williams who lived with Roger Top. Acquaint Mr.
Carmack that his son was slightly wounded thro the
shoulder and arm & that he is in a likely way of
Recovery we leave him at mouth of Canaway & one

Very Careful hand to take care of him; there is a
garrison & three hundred men left at that place with
a surgeon to Heal the wounded we Expect to Return
to the Garrison in about 16 days from the Shawny
Towns.

I have nothing more Perticular to Acquaint you
with Concerning the Battle, as to the Country I
cant now say much in praise of any that I have yet
seen. Dady intended writing to you but did not know
of the Express til the time was too short I have wrote
to Mam(b)y tho not so fully as to you as I then
Expected the Express was just going, we seem to be
all in a moving Posture Just going from this place
so that I must Conclude wishing you health and
prosperity till I see you & Your Family in the meantime I am yr. truly Effectionate_Friend & Humble
servt. ISAAC SHELBY.

Major Lewis with the best of his troops
joined Lord Dunmore a few days after the
battle. The combined forces crossed the Ohio
and destroyed a number of Indian towns.
This had the desired effect as the Indians
soon begged for peace. The battle of the
Great Kanawha may be classed as one of the
most decisive Indian battles ever fought on
American soil. The results achieved were
far-reaching. The incursions of the northern
Indians were stopped. The frontiersmen
were released for service in the Revolution
and against the Cherokees on the south.

It was in this battle that the frontiersmen first used the Indian method of fighting to any great extent. The success of the expedition inspired the settlers with new courage and the experience gained in this battle was responsible for the defeat of the Indians at Long Island (Kingsport) in July, 1776.

While infrequent raids were made into the Holston Valleys as late as 1795, never at any time were the settlers in danger of being wiped out as they were prior to the battle of Point Pleasant.

SKETCH SEVEN
The Cherokees on the Warpath

The Cherokees on the Warpath

IN the spring of 1775 the old fort at Long Island was repaired and the name changed to Fort Patrick Henry. Seeing that war with the Colonies was inevitable, Alexander Cameron and John Stewart, British agents among the Cherokees, proceeded by bribes and every means in their power to enlist the Cherokee Indians on the side of the crown. At first the Indians were incredulous, as they could not believe that the white men would take up arms against each other. Civil war among Indians of the same tribe and who spoke the same language was unknown. Cameron finally enlisted the Indians by promising them many presents and freedom to plunder and take scalps at will. The Cherokees had long resented the encroachment of the whites upon their hunting grounds and were pleased to have any excuse to go on the warpath. In the spring of 1776 the war drums sounded throughout the

nation. Had it not been for the timely
warning given by Nancy Ward in June of
this year, it is very probable the Holston
settlements would have been entirely destroyed. Like a red pestilence the invasion,
led by Dragging Canoe and Abraham, swept
up the Holston Valley seven hundred strong.
Hurriedly word was sent to the settlers of
Carter's Valley and they hastened to the
protection of Eaton's Station, seven miles
east of Kingsport at the foot of Eden's Ridge.
A small force of soldiers had already gathered
and a fort was hurriedly constructed from
the materials at hand. Scouts were sent out
to summon help and companies from Black's
Fort at Abingdon and Shelby's Fort at
Bristol hastened to their aid. In a short
time one hundred and seventy-five frontiersmen were assembled and word was brought
that the Indians were advancing from the
direction of Long Island. A council of war
was held and it was decided to advance and
meet the foe in open battle. The Indians
rarely attacked a well garrisoned fort and it
was feared they would turn aside and go
through the settlements murdering the de-
fenseless women and children, while their

Typical Frontier Fort and Stockade

(Of such construction was Fort Patrick Henry at Kingsport)

husbands and fathers remained in the fort impotent to protect them.

Oliver Taylor states in "Historic Sullivan" that it was on the advice of William Cocke, who was captain of one of the Sullivan County companies, that they came forth and prepared to meet the enemy. They proceeded to Long Island Flats where the advance guard met about twenty Indians coming toward the fort. These were fired upon and pursued some distance. As all of the frontiersmen had not arrived it was decided to fall back on the fort. The retreat had not proceeded far when they were overtaken and attacked by a band of some three hundred warriors under Dragging Canoe. The whites immediately formed a battle line and met the onslaught with equal fury.

Many of the frontiersmen in this battle were veterans of the Point Pleasant campaign and were familiar with the Indian method of fighting. Adopting the red man's tactics they were more than a match for him. Many deeds of individual valor were performed in this battle and the defeat of the Indians gave renewed courage to the frontiersmen, who now felt confident they could defend their homes successfully and maintain their titles to the lands they had suffered so much for. The official account of the battle is very interesting and is given in full:

OFFICIAL REPORT OF THE BATTLE OF ISLAND FLATS

On the 19th our scouts returned, and informed us that they had discovered where a great number of Indians were making into the settlements, upon which alarm the few men stationed at Eaton's completed a breast-work sufficiently strong, with the assistance of what men were there, to have repelled a considerable number; sent expresses to the different stations and collected all the forces in one body, and the morning after about one hundred and seventy turned out in search of the enemy. We marched in two divisions, with flankers on each side and scouts before. Our scouts discovered upwards of twenty meeting us, and fired on them. They returned the fire, but our men rushed on them with such violence that they were obliged to make a precipitate retreat. We took ten bundles and a good deal of plunder, and had great reason to think some of them were wounded. This small skirmish happened on ground very disadvantageous for our men to pursue, though it was with the greatest difficulty our officers could restrain their men. A council was held, and it was thought advisable to return, as we imagined there was a large party not far off. We accordingly returned, and had not marched more than a mile when a number, not inferior to ours, attacked us in the rear. Our men

sustained the attack with great bravery and intrepidity, immediately forming a line. The Indians endeavored to surround us, but were prevented by the
uncommon fortitude and vigilance of Capt. James
Shelby who took possession of an eminence that
prevented their design. Our line of battle extended
about a quarter of a mile. We killed about thirteen
on the spot, whom we found, and we have the greatest
reason to believe that we could have found a great
many more had we had time to search for them.
There were streams of blood every way, and it was
generally thought there was never so much execution
done in so short a time on the frontiers. Never did
troops fight with greater calmness than ours did. The
Indians attacked us with the greatest fury imaginable,
and made the most vigorous efforts to surround us.
Our spies really deserve the greatest applause. We
took a great deal of plunder and many guns, and had
only four men greatly wounded. The rest of the
troops are in high spirits and eager for another engagement. We have the greatest reason to believe
they are pouring in great numbers on us, and beg the
assistance of our friends.

James Thompson,	John Campbell,
James Shelby,	William Cocke,
William Buchanan,	Thomas Madison.

To Maj. Anthony Bledsoe, for him to be immediately sent to Col. Preston.

While the attack was being made on the
Virginia settlements by Dragging Canoe,
another band of Cherokees under Abraham
had gone up the Holston and Watauga

rivers and attacked the Watauga settlements near what is now the town of Elizabethton, Tennessee. Fortunately the whites had sufficient warning to enable them to take refuge in the fort, where they were besieged for three weeks. The erection of Black's Fort at Abingdon was begun on July 30, the same day that the battle of Long Island Flats was fought. The defeat at Long Island did not end the Indian troubles on the Virginia frontiers. Black's Fort, at Abingdon, Virginia, had scarcely been completed and furnished refuge for nearly five hundred people, when straggling bands of the Cherokees appeared in the immediate vicinity. Foraging parties were waylaid and attacked, and the Rev. Charles Cummings barely escaped death when his party of four were fired on at about a mile distant from the fort, on Pipers Hill, a suburb of Abingdon, Virginia. William Creswell was killed and was the first person to be buried in the Abingdon Cemetery. His grave is marked by a granite monument. The home of Captain James Montgomery on the south fork of the Holston was plundered and burned, the family having taken refuge

in Black's Fort. In retaliation Captain Montgomery, learning of the camping place of
this same band, on the upper waters of the
Holston, pursued them with a small company of men from Black's Fort. They were
joined by a party from Bryan's Fort and the
Indian camp was quietly surrounded during
the night. At the dawn of day when the
Indians first began to stir, the whites opened
a deadly fire and killed eleven of the enemy.
The rest of the party took to the river, where
they were picked off like floating turtles. Of
this party of Cherokees numbering more
than twenty, only one escaped to return to
his home at Chickamauga.

While these marauding parties were scat-
tered over the Holston and Clinch Valleys,
the fort at Watauga was still under siege
and its crowded occupants undergoing great
hardships. The Rev. Charles Cummings
organized about one hundred of his parish-
ioners at Black's Fort and under the command of Colonel Evan Shelby hastened to
the relief of the Watauga settlements (Fort
Lee). As a result of this inroad of the
Cherokees, Col. William Christian, Capt.
William Campbell and Capt. William Russell

obtained leave of absence from the Continental Army and returned to the defense of their homes on the frontier.

SKETCH EIGHT
The State of Franklin

The State of Franklin

THE Watauga settlements, in the neighborhood of what is now the city of Elizabethton, were among the earliest in this section. The pioneers who located in the beautiful valleys of the Watauga and Nolichucky rivers were the same type of hardy Scotch-Irish as those who first settled the Holston Valleys. All of what is now northeast Tennessee was supposed to be in Virginia, but was too far removed from the seat of government at Williamsburg for the infant settlement to derive any assistance from the parent. This did not disturb the resourceful pioneers, for we find them in 1772 gathered in solemn conclave for the purpose of establishing a government of their own. These articles were duly promulgated as the "Articles of the Watauga Association." McLaughlin says:

One can find no more striking fact in American History, nor one more typical, than the simple ease

with which the frontiersmen on the banks of the
western waters, on the threshold of the central valley
of the continent, finding themselves beyond the pale
of Eastern law, formed an association and exercised
the rights and privileges of self-government.

This little settlement was frequently harassed by the Indians and the settlers were
compelled to defend their lives and property
from the portals of their fort. Despite the
constant fear of Indian attack the Watauga
settlements always contributed men to every
important campaign that was for the good
of the entire section. After the correct
boundary was established between North
Carolina and Virginia the Watauga Association petitioned the North Carolina Assembly
to be permitted to come under its protection,
July 5, 1776.

Strange as it may seem, the genesis of the
Franklin movement started with a Virginian.
Colonel Arthur Campbell was among the
earliest pioneers of the Holston Valleys. His
father, Colonel David Campbell, was a member of the Walker expedition in 1746. He
entered a large tract of land and settled at
Royal Oak, now Marion, Virginia. Arthur
Campbell was well educated for the times

and was a ready and daring leader and had
served his county and state in many capacities. Realizing how remote the Holston
settlements were from the central government he conceived the idea of a separate
state to be composed of the five southwestern
counties of Virginia and the counties of
Washington and Sullivan in North Carolina.
Early in 1782 he issued a document calling
for a Convention of Delegates to be held at
Abingdon, Virginia, to ascertain the sense
of the people as to joining this movement.
There is no record that an election was ever
held for the election of deputies to the convention called to meet at Abingdon. General
William Russell of Virginia heartily opposed
the movement and preferred charges against
Colonel Campbell before the Virginia Assembly. So nearly divided was the balance
of power between these two prominent
leaders that Colonel Arthur Campbell was
compelled to desist in his active efforts to
form a new state as outlined in his call for a
convention in 1782. The seed planted by
him, however, quickly sprouted and took
root across the border in Tennessee. Interest
in favor of the separation movement grew,

and gave no little concern to the statesmen
in Virginia and North Carolina.

The Continental Congress in 1780 resolved
that, if the trans-Alleghany country owned
by Virginia, North Carolina and Georgia be
ceded to the government, this territory be
laid out in separate states at such times and
in such manner as Congress should thereafter
direct. That such new states be republican
in form and have the same rights of sovereignty as the other states.

This assertion on the part of Congress was
construed by the pioneers on the waters of
the Holston and Watauga to have been a
declaration of sovereignty over the western
country and the purpose to create new states.
In 1784 the legislature of North Carolina
ceded the western country to the Federal
government. The delegates to the North
Carolina Assembly of 1784, from the mountain counties of Sullivan, Washington, Greene
and Davidson, all voted for the Cessation Act.

The transmountain section had derived
practically no benefit from the home government. The state of North Carolina was
burdened with debt and in no position even
to protect her frontiers. Under these condi-

tions it was perfectly natural that the frontiersmen of this section should set about establishing an independent government of their own.

The first General Assembly of the state of Franklin was held at Jonesboro in March, 1785. John Sevier was elected the first governor despite the fact that he had at first been opposed to the separatist movement. Landon Carter was first Speaker of the Senate and Thomas Talbot its clerk. William Cage was elected Speaker of the House of Commons and Thomas Chapman, clerk. David Campbell, a brother of Colonel Arthur Campbell of Virginia, was elected Judge of the Superior Court and Joshua Fist and John Anderson assistant judges. Owing to the fact that there was not a printing press west of the Blue Ridge Mountains the laws of the state of Franklin were never published. One of the first acts was "An act for the promotion of learning in the county of Washington (Tenn.). Under this act Martin's Academy was reincorporated. This institution had been founded by Rev. Samuel Doak in 1780, near Jonesboro. On motion of John Sevier a charter was granted to the institution under

the name of Washington College. It was
the first educational institution founded west
of the mountains and has been in existence
ever since.

The four years of the state of Franklin
were few and full of trouble. Governor
Martin of North Carolina had naught but
displeasure for the new state and by mani-
festo and proclamation endeavored to block
the progress of the new ship of state. The
matter of the right to set up a new state was
even carried to the Continental Congress.
William Cocke carried a memorial from the
Assembly of Franklin to the Continental
Congress in session in New York and presented the same May 16, 1785. This memorial petitioned Congress to admit the state
of Franklin into the sisterhood of sovereign
states.

During the years 1786–87 chaos reigned in
the new state of Franklin. North Carolina
had never resigned her right of sovereignty
over the territory west of the mountains and
we have the strange spectacle of two governments attempting to function over the same
people. County courts were held in the same
counties under both governments. Civil

officers and the militia of both states attempted to function and taxes were levied by both governments. The several officials came into daily conflict and personal prowess was the chief qualification for the office of sheriff or constable. Colonel John Tipton had remained loyal to the state of North Carolina and as representative of that state held rival courts in the state of Franklin. At one time Colonel Tipton and Governor John Sevier met in the streets of Jonesboro and so great was the animosity existing that they speedily came to blows.

On one occasion, while the Sevier Court was in session at Jonesboro, Tipton at the head of a small army entered the courthouse, turned out all of the magistrates and took possession of the papers. Later Sevier, in like manner, returned the party call, ousted the officials and retook the papers, which his brother Valentine Sevier hid in a cave. In this way many valuable records, both of marriages and deeds, were destroyed or lost, causing confusion and litigation in after years. ("Historic Sullivan")

Colonel Tipton was of a very fiery temperament and was the persistent enemy of the new government. Loyal to his state and jealous of the new movement, he looked upon the action of Sevier and his followers as high treason. This precipitated a small civil war. Sevier being absent from home on the frontier fighting Indians, Colonel Tipton caused the seizure of a number of Sevier's slaves to satisfy an execution issued in North Carolina. Word of the seizure having reached Sevier he hastened home and at the head of one hundred and fifty of his followers marched on Tipton's stronghold, which was his home. Tipton hurriedly summoned a number of his adherents and barricaded his home, which was about one and a half miles from the present Johnson City, Tennessee. Sevier, having brought along a small cannon, took advantage of a slight eminence overlooking Tipton's home and demanded the surrender of Tipton and all of his men. A vitriolic reply from Tipton was received and he in turn demanded Sevier to surrender under the law of North Carolina.

In the meantime Tipton had sent out runners for reinforcements. Sevier settled down for a siege of Tipton's house and ordered all avenues of escape guarded. Answering Tipton's summons Colonel Maxwell and Colonel Pemberton had collected a body of men in Sullivan County and rendezvoused at Dunn-

gan's on the Holston. Next morning they
were at Tipton's by sunrise. The troops,
under Maxwell, fired a volley and gave a
battle cry not surpassed by the Indians.
Tipton's forces sallied forth from the house
and the Sevier forces were forced to retreat
to a higher position. Many shots were
exchanged during a blinding snowstorm, but
only one man was killed and a few wounded.
The Sevier forces retreated toward Jonesboro.
An armistice was entered into the next day
and civil war was barely averted.

Two of Sevier's sons, John, Jr., and James,
were absent on a scouting expedition during the battle at Tipton's house. Coming
up later they were captured by Tipton's men
and only by the intervention of some of his
young officers was Tipton prevented from
having the young men hung.

Colonel Joseph Martin had been appointed
successor to General Evan Shelby in command of the forces west of the mountains.
He set about bringing peace to the distracted
state of Franklin and in a measure succeeded.
Indian depredations from various quarters
occupied the entire attention of Governor
John Sevier and General Martin. Colonel

Tipton's influence had declined with the election of General Martin. Sevier's term of office had expired and interest in the new state lagged. Judge Samuel Williams in the "Lost State of Franklin" says:

At the February term (1789) of the Greene County Court, John Sevier, Joseph Hardin, Henry Conway and Hugh Wear, came into court and took the oath of allegiance, agreeable to the Act of the Assembly, in such cases made and provided. Then truly the State of Franklin had come to an end. Governor Caswell's policy of conciliation had at last vindicated itself, and it continued to be the policy of the Mother State until the second session act was passed.

First Declaration of Independence

First Declaration of Independence

PRIOR to the year 1775 all of southwest Virginia from the Blue Ridge Mountains westward was known as Fincastle County. This huge territory was abolished as the county of Fincastle by the General Assembly of Virginia in October, 1776. Out of its territory were created the counties of Kentucky, Washington and Montgomery.

The first Declaration of Independence was declared by the frontiersmen of Fincastle County. On January 20, 1775, the freemen of Fincastle County assembled at the lead mines and made a declaration which was the precursor of that of July 4, 1776, made by the Congress at Philadelphia. This declaration of the Fincastle men, foreshadowing American Independence, was the first one made in America, and it so fully breathes the spirit of independence and freedom that it is here inserted in full:*

"In obedience to the resolves of the Continental Congress a meeting of the freeholders of Fincastle County, in Virginia, was held on the 20th day of January, 1775, and who, after approving of the association formed by that august body in behalf of all of the colonies, and subscribing thereto, proceeded to the election of a committee, to see the same carried punctually into execution, when the following gentlemen were nominated:

"The Reverend Charles Cummings, Colonel William Preston, Colonel William Christian, Captain Stephen Trigg, Major Arthur Campbell, Major William Ingles, Captain James McGavock, Captain Walter Crockett, Captain John Montgomery, Captain William Campbell, Captain Thomas Madison, Captain Evan Shelby and Lieutenant William Edmondson. After the election, the committee made choice of Colonel William Christian for their chairman, and appointed Mr. David Campbell to be clerk.

"The following address was then unani-

*From the American Archives, 4th Series, 1st Volume, page 1166.

mously agreed to by the people of the County and is as follows:

To the Honourable Peyton Randolph, Esquire, Richard Henry Lee, George Washington, Patrick Henry, Junior, Richard Bland, Benjamin Harrison, and Edmund Pendleton, Esquires, the delegates from this colony who attended the Continental Congress held at Philadelphia: Gentlemen: Had it not been for our remote situation, and the Indian war which we were lately engaged in, to chastise these cruel and savage people for the many murders and depredations they have committed amongst us, now happily terminated under the auspices of our present worthy Governor, his Excellency, the Right Honourable Earl of Dunmore, we should have before this time made known to you our thankfulness for the very important services you have rendered to your country, in conjunction with the worthy delegates from the other provinces. Your noble efforts for reconciling the mother country and the colonies, on rational and constitutional principles, and your pasifick, steady and uniform conduct in that arduous work, immortalize you in the annals of your country. We heartily concur in your resolutions and shall, in every instance, strictly and invariably adhere thereto.

We assure you, gentlemen, and all our countrymen, that we are a people whose hearts overflow with love and duty to our lawful Sovereign George the Third, whose illustrious House for several successive reigns have been the guardians of the civil and religious rights and liberties of British subjects, as settled at the glorious revolution; that we are willing to risk our lives in the service of his Majesty for the support of the Protestant Religion, and the rights and liberties of his subjects as they have been established by compact, Law and Ancient Charters. We are heartily grieved at the differences which now subsist between the parent state and the colonies, and most urgently wish to see harmony restored on an equitable basis, and by the most lenient measures that can be devised by the heart of man. Many of us and our forefathers left our native land, considering it as a Kingdom subjected to inordinate power; we crossed the Atlantic and explored this then wilderness, bordering on many Natives or Savages and surrounded by mountains almost inaccessible to any but those various Savages, who have insistantly been committing depredations on us since our first settling the Country. These fatigues and dangers were patiently encountered, supported by the pleasing hope of enjoying these rights and liberties which had been granted to Virginians, and denied us in our native country, and of transmitting them inviolate to our posterity; but even to this remote region the hand of enmity and unconstitutional power hath proceeded us to strip of that liberty and property with which God, Natures, and the Rights of Humanity have visited us. We are ready and willing to contribute all in our power for the support of his Majesty's Government if applied to considerately, and when grants are made by our own Representatives, but cannot think of submitting our liberty or property to the power of a venial British Parliament, or the will of a greedy ministry.

We by no means desire to shake off our duty or allengians to our lawful Sovereign, but on the contrary shall ever glory in being the royal subjects of the Protestant Prince, descended from such illustrious progenitors, so long as we can enjoy the free exercise of our religion as Protestants and of our liberties and properties as British subjects. But if no pacific measures shall be proposed or adopted by Great Britain, and our enemies will attempt to dragoon us out of these inestimable privileges which we are entitled to as subjects, and to reduce us to a state of slavery, we declare that we are deliberately determined never to surrender them to any power upon earth but at the expense of our lives.

These are real though unpolished sentiments of liberty, and in them we are resolved to live or die.

We are, gentlemen, with the most perfect esteem and regard,

Your most obedient servants."

SKETCH TEN
Laws Framed By Our Forefathers

SKETCH TEN

Laws Framed By Our Forefathers

IF we are fully to understand the nature and character of the pioneers of this section it is necessary that we give some consideration to the laws under which they lived at that time. A study of the "Public Acts of the General Assembly" and ordinances of the Conventions of Virginia passed since the year 1768, reveals some very interesting laws. Many of these may seem to be cruel and heartless, but they were a product of the times during which the lawmakers lived. It is noteworthy, however, that the majority of the laws were founded on the fundamentals of equity and justice, and that these same laws, with slight modifications, are on our very latest statute books. In the year 1769 we find the constituted authorities taking cognizance of the growth of gambling throughout the Colonies and the following act was passed:

At a General Assembly, begun and held at the Capitol in the City of Williamsburg, on Tuesday, the 7th day of November, Anno Domini, 1769, in the 10th year of the reign of George III, of Great Britain, France and Ireland, King, Defender of the Faith, etc.

CHAPTER XVII OF VA. ASSEMBLY

An act for preventing and suppressing private lotteries. Whereas many pernicious games, called lotteries, have been set up in this colony, which have a manifest tendency toward the corruption of morals, and the impoverishment of families; and whereas such pernicious practices may not only give opportunity to defraud the honest and industrious, but may be productive of all manner of vice, idleness and immorality, and against the common good and welfare of the community; For remedy whereof, Be it enacted by the Governor, council, and burgesses, of the present General Assembly, and it is hereby enacted by the authority of the same, that from and after the first day of May, next, no person or persons, whatever, shall, on his own account, or that of another, either publicly or privately, set up, erect, expose, or cause to be played, drawn or thrown at, any such lotteries, or shall procure the same to be done, either by dice, lots, cards, tickets, or any other number or figures, or any other way whatever; and every person or persons herein offending, shall forfeit and pay to the parish, for the use of the poor of such parish, where such offense shall be committed, the whole of the sum or sums to be raised by such lottery; to be recovered by action of debt, or information in any court within this colony.

There are thousands of intelligent people in our vast country to-day who are opposed to vaccination in any form and especially against the compulsory vaccination for smallpox. Among this number are many scientists and noted physicians. Laws requiring compulsory vaccination are on the statute books of many of our states to-day. Viewed in the light of another century of progress, these laws will seem to be as ignorant and unproductive of good as the inoculation practiced by the pioneers nearly two centuries ago. Evidence that there were progressive thinkers in those days will be found in the next act of the same Assembly. In Chapter XXVI we find the following:

An act to regulate the inoculation of the small-pox within this Colony:

Whereas the wanton introduction of the small-pox into this colony by inoculation, when the same was not necessary, hath, of late years, proved a nuisance to several neighborhoods, by disturbing the peace and quiet of many of his Majesty's subjects, and exposing their lives to the effects of that mortal distemper, which from the situation and circumstances of the Colony, they would otherwise have little reason to dread. To prevent which for the future, Be it enacted, &c., that if any person or persons whatever, shall wilfully or designedly, after the first day of September next ensuing, presume to import or bring into this colony, from any country or place whatever, the small-pox, or any varilous or infectious matter of the said distemper, with the purpose of inoculating any person or persons whatever, or by any means whatever, to propagate the said distemper within this colony, he or she, so offending, shall forfeit or pay the sum of one thousand pounds, for every offence so committed; one moiety whereof shall be to the informer, and the other moiety to the church wardens of the parish, where the offence shall be committed, for the use of the poor of said parish.

One of the most remarkable acts that has ever been placed on the statute books of any state or country was an act passed by the Virginia legislature on December 16, 1785.

This act was written by Thomas Jefferson and has never been changed in the slightest respect from that day to this. It is embodied in the Code of Virginia and was reaffirmed by the Legislature of 1919. The text of the act given below is an exact copy taken from the original edition of the Acts of the Assembly printed in 1794. The entire act contains 546 words and is a single sentence. While it is expressed in quaint old English, no statute has ever been written which more clearly expresses the fundamental principles of religious freedom. No hand has

ever been raised in the Virginia legislature
to repeal it.

AN ACT FOR ESTABLISHING
RELIGIOUS FREEDOM

(Passed the 16th of December, 1785)

1. Whereas Almighty God hath created the mind
free; that all attempts to influence it by temporal
punishments or burthens, or by civil incapacitations,
tend only to beget habits of hypocrisy and measures,
and are a departure from the plan of the Holy Author
of our religion, who being Lord both of body and
mind, yet chose not to propagate it by coercion on
either as was in his Almighty power to do; that the
impious presumption of Legislators and Rulers, civil
as well as ecclesiastical, who being themselves but
fallible and uninspired men, have assumed dominion
over the faith of others, setting up their own opinions
and modes of thinking as the only true and infallible,
and as such endeavoring to impose them on others,
hath established and maintained false religions over
the greatest part of the world, and through all time;
that to compel a man to furnish contributions of
money for the propagations of opinions which he
disbelieves, is sinful and tyrannical, that even forcing
him to support this or that teacher of his own religious persuasion, is depriving him of the comfortable
liberty of giving his contributions to the particular
pastor, whose morals he would make his pattern, and
whose powers he feels most persuasive to righteous-
ness, and is withdrawing from the ministry those
temporary rewards, which proceeding from an appro-
bation of their personal conduct, are an additional
incitement to earnest and unremitting labours for the

instruction of mankind; that our civil rights have no dependence on our religious opinions, any more than our opinions in physics or geometry; that therefore the proscribing of any Citizen as unworthy the public confidence, by laying upon him an incapacity of being called to offices of trust and emolument, unless he profess or renounce this or that religious opinion, is depriving him injuriously, of privileges and advantages, to which in common with his fellow-citizens he has a natural right; that it tends only to corrupt the principles of that religion it is meant to encourage, by bribing with a monoply of worldly honors and emolument, those who will externally profess and conform to it, that though these indeed are criminal who do not withstand such temptations, yet neither are those innocent who lay the bait in their way; that to suffer the civil magistrate to intrude his powers into the field of opinion, and to restrain the profession of propagation of principles on supposition of their ill tendency, is a dangerous fallacy, which at once destroys all religious liberty, because he, being of course judge of that tendency, will make his opinions the rule of judgment, and approve or condemn the sentiments of others, only as they shall square with or differ from his own; that it is time enough for the rightful purpose of civil government, for its officers to interfere when principles break out into overt acts against peace and good order; and finally that truth is great and will prevail if left to herself; that she is the proper and sufficient antagonist to error, and has nothing to fear from the conflict, unless by human interposition disarmed of her natural weapons, free argument and debate, ere ceasing to be dangerous, when it is permitted freely to contradict them,

2. Be it enacted by the General Assembly that no man shall be compelled to frequent or support any religious worship, place of Ministry, nor shall be enforced, registered, molested, or burthened in his body or goods, nor shall otherwise suffer on account of his religious opinion or belief; but that all men shall be free to profess and by argument to maintain, their opinions in matters of religion, and that the fame shall in no wise diminish, enlarge or affect their civil capacities.

The early colonists believed that if a man were not naturally religious he should be made so by law. This is evidenced by the Acts of the Assembly, 1705, which placed a heavy penalty upon nonobservers of the Sabbath day, and for profane swearing or drunkenness. If the offender could not produce a sufficient amount of tobacco to pay his fine he could be publicly whipped, as an alternative.

Be it enacted and it is hereby enacted by the authorities aforesaid, that if any person, being of the age of twenty-one years, or upward, shall wilfully absent him or herself from divine service at his or her Parish Church or Chapel, the space of one month, (excepting as is passed in the first year of King William and Queen Mary, entitled an act for exempting their Majesties' protestant subjects dissenting from the Church of England from the penalties of certain laws), and shall not, when there, in a decent and orderly manner continue until the said service is ended, and if any person shall on that day be present at any disorderly meeting, gaming or tippling, or shall on the said day make any journey, and travel upon the road, except to and from church, (cases of necessity and charity excepted), or shall on the said day be found working in their corn or tobacco, or any other labour of their ordinary calling other than is necessary for the sustenance of man and beast; every person failing or making default in any of the premises, and being lawfully convicted, by confession, or otherwise, before one or more justice or justices of the peace of the county wherein such offences shall be committed (so that prosecution be made within two months after such default) shall forfeit and pay for every such offence, the sum of five shillings or fifty pounds of tobacco. And if any person or persons herein offending shall refuse to make present payment, or give sufficient caution for the payment of the fine at the laying of the next parish levy after such offence committed, each party so offending, and not paying or giving security as aforesaid, shall be, receive on his or her bare back ten lashes, well laid on.

AN ACT FOR THE EFFECTUAL SUPPRESSION OF VICE, AND RESTRAINT AND PUNISHMENT OF BLAS-PHEMOUS, WICKED, AND DISSOLUTE PERSONS. (PASSED OCT., 1705)

Be it enacted by the Governor, council, and bur-gesses, of this present General Assembly, and it is hereby enacted by the authority of the same, that if any person or persons brought up in the Christian Religion, shall by writing, printing, teaching, or advisedly speaking, deny the Being of a God of the Holy Trinity, or shall assert or maintain there are more Gods than one, or shall deny the Christian Religion to be true, or the holy Scriptures of the Old and New Testaments not to be of divine authority, and be thereof lawfully convicted, upon indictment, or information, in the general court of this, her Majesty's Colony and Dominion, such person or persons, for the first offence, shall be adjudged incapable, or disable in law, to all intents and purposes whatsoever, to hold, enjoy any office or employment, ecclesiastical, civil, or military, or any part in them, or any profit or advantage to them appertaining, or any of them and if any person or persons so convicted as aforesaid shall, at any time of his or their conviction, enjoy or possess any office, place or employment, such office, place or employment, shall be void, and is hereby declared void. And if such person or persons shall be a second time lawfully convicted, as aforesaid, of all or any of the crimes aforesaid, that then he, she, or they, shall from henceforth be disabled to sue, prosecute, plead or use any action or information in any court of law or equity, or to be guardian to any child, or to be executor, or administrator of any person or capable of deed of gift or legacy, or to bear any office civil or military, forever, within this, her Majesty's colony and dominion; and shall also suffer from the time of such conviction, three years imprisonment, without bail or mainprize.

And be it further enacted, by the authority aforesaid, and it is hereby enacted, that if any person or persons shall profanely swear or curse, or shall be drunk, he, she, or they, so offending, for every such offence, being thereof convicted by the oath of one or more witnesses (which oath any justice of the peace is hereby empowered and required to administer) or by confession before one or more justice or justices of the peace in the county where such offence shall be committed, shall forfeit and pay the sum of five shillings or fifty pounds of tobacco, for every such offence; or if the offence or offences be committed in the presence or hearing of one or more justice or justices of the peace or in any court of record in this her Majesty's colony and dominion, the same shall be a sufficient conviction, without any other evidence; and the said offender shall, upon such conviction, forfeit and pay the sum of five shillings or fifty pounds of tobacco, for every such offence. And if any person or persons shall refuse to make present payment or give sufficient caution for the payment of the same, at the laying of the next parish levy after the said offence committed, then the said fines and penalties shall be levied upon the goods of such person or persons, by warrant or precept from any justice of peace before whom the same conviction shall be; which warrant may be directed to the sheriff of the county, or to the constable in his respective precinct, to be appraised and valued, as in other distresses, and if the offender or offenders be not able to pay the said sum or sums, then he, she, or they shall have and receive ten lashes upon his or her bare back, well laid on, for every such offence.

Patrick Henry, in his famous speech in the "Parson's Cause," was the first speaker in America to voice the truth that government exists only by consent of the governed; that law is but the crystallized opinion of the people—that the voice of the people is the voice of God. In that famous speech Patrick Henry committed himself irrevocably to the principle of human rights.

The decade preceeding the Revolutionary War was full of static. Mutterings and rumblings were heard even from distant New England; they rolled down the coast, up through the Piedmont section, across the Blue Ridge and down into the Holston Valleys. The frontier people of southwest Virginia and east Tennessee had carved out a home in the wilderness that they might enjoy those human rights which Patrick Henry had advocated.

So in 1775, month of January, we find the representatives of the mountain people in meeting assembled to declare their right of self-government and religious freedom. Following the old Scotch custom they made their Dominie, the Rev. Chas. Cummins, the chairman of the meeting, and drafted the Fincastle Resolutions. This was the first Declaration of Independence ever passed by the American Colonists, and was the forerunner of the Bill of Rights.

Patrick Henry, who first kindled the fires of freedom in Virginia, was distinctly a frontier type, rough and uncouth in his manner and appearance. His own family little dreamed that he would ever become an orator and leader.

Thomas Jefferson was the exact opposite, an aristocrat by birth and training, an educated and polished scholar. He was fully equipped by education and natural endowments to be the author of the written declarations of the Colonists when their patience with tyranny and injustice had reached the limit.

Jefferson was the author of the Virginia Declaration of Rights passed by the Virginia Assembly May 6, 1776, two months before the Declaration of Independence was passed at Philadelphia. This was one of the three great documents that Jefferson wrote and, recognizing this fact, he asked to have inscribed on his monument: "Thomas Jefferson, author of the Declaration of Rights, Declaration of Independence, The Statute of Religious Freedom."

At a general convention of delegates and representatives from the several counties and corporation of Virginia, held at the Capitol in the city of Williamsburg on Monday,

May 6, 1776, the following Declaration was passed:

A Declaration of Rights made by the Representatives of the great people of Virginia, assembled in full and free convention, which rights do pertain to them and their posterity as the basis and foundation of their government.

1. That all men are equally free and independent and have certain inherent rights, of which, when they enter into a state of society they cannot, by any compact, deprive or divest their posterity, namely, the enjoyment of life and liberty, with the means of acquiring and possessing prosperity and pursuing and obtaining happiness and safety.

2. That all power is vested in, and consequently derived from the people; that magistrates are their trustees and servants, and at all times amenable to them.

3. That government is, or ought to be, instituted for the common benefit, protection and security of the people, nation or community; of all the various forms and modes of the government, that is best, which is capable of producing the greatest degree of happiness and safety, and is most effectually secured against the danger of mal-administration; and that when any government shall be found inadequate or contrary to these purposes a majority of the community hath an indubitable, unalienable and indefeasible right to reform, or alter or abolish it in such manner as shall be judged most conducive to the public weal.

4. That no man or set of men are entitled to exclusive or separate emoluments or privileges from the

community, but in consideration of public services, which not being descendable, neither ought the offices of magistrates, legislator, or judge to be hereditary.

5. That the legislative and executive powers of the state should be separate and distinct from the judiciary; and that the members of the first may be restrained from oppression by feeling and participating the burdens of the people. They should, at fixed periods, be reduced to a private station, returning to that body from which they were originally taken, and the vacancies be supplied by frequent, certain, and regular elections, in which all or any part of the former members, to be again eligible, or ineligible, as the laws may direct.

6. That elections of members to serve as representatives of the people, in Assembly, ought to be free, and that all men, having sufficient evidence of permanent common interest, with an attachment to community, have the right of suffrage and cannot be taxed or deprived of their property for public uses without their own consent, or that of their representatives so elected, nor bound by any law to which they have not in like manner assented, for the public good.

7. That all power of suspending laws or execution of laws by any authority without consent of the representatives of the people is injurious to their rights and ought not to be exercised.

8. That in all capital, or criminal prosecutions a man hath a right to demand the cause and nature of his accusation, to be confronted with his accusers and witnesses, to call for evidence in his favor, and to a speedy trial by an impartial jury of his vicinage, without whose unanimous consent he cannot be found guilty, nor can he be compelled to give evidence

against himself; that no man be deprived of his liberty except by the law of the land or the judgment of his peers.

9. That excessive bail ought not to be required nor excessive fines imposed, nor cruel and unusual punishment inflicted.

10. That general warrants, whereby an officer or messenger may be commanded to search suspected places without evidence of a fact committed, ought to seize any person or persons not named, or whose offence is not particularly described and supported by evidence, are grievous and oppressive, and ought not to be granted.

11. That in controversy respecting property and suits between man and man, the ancient trial by jury is preferable to any other, and ought to be held sacred.

12. That the freedom of the press is one of the great bulwarks of liberty and can never be restrained but by despotic governments.

13. That a well regulated militia, composed of the body of the people, trained to arms, is the proper, natural, and safe defence of a free state; that standing armies, in time of peace, should be avoided, as dangerous to liberty; and that in all cases the military should be under strict subordination to and governed by the civil power.

14. That the people have a right to uniform government, and therefore, that no government separate from or independent of the government of Virginia ought to be erected or established within the limits thereof.

15. That no free government or the blessing of liberty can be preserved to any people but by a firm adherence to justice, moderation, temperance, frugal-

ity and virtue and by frequent recurrence to fundamental principles.

16. That religion, or the duty that we owe our
Creator and the manner of discharging it can be
directed only by reason and conviction, not by force
or violence, and therefore all men are equally entitled
to the free exercise of religion, according to the
dictates of conscience; and that it is the mutual duty
of all to practise Christian forbearance, love and
charity towards each other.

The qualifications required of the citizens
of Fincastle County, Virginia, to vote and
hold office in 1776, the last year that the
colony of Virginia adhered to the crown of
England, follow.

The freeholders of every county possessed
the liberty of electing two of the most able
and fit men, being freeholders and qualified
to vote, to represent their county in all the
General Assemblies. The electors or voters
were required to own an estate or freehold
for their own life or the life of another, or
other greater estate in at least fifty acres of
land, if no settlement be made upon it, or
twenty-five acres with a plantation and
house thereon at least twelve feet square,
said property being in the county in which
the electors offered to vote. The sheriff was

required to deliver to the minister and reader of every parish in his county a copy of the writ of election, and upon the back of every such writ he was required to indorse the fact that said election would be held at the courthouse in his county upon a day appointed by him. And the minister or reader was required to publish the same immediately after divine services every Sunday between the receipt of said writ and the day of election, under heavy penalty for failure to do so. It was further provided that every freeholder actually residing in the county should personally appear at the courthouse on the day fixed and give his vote, upon the penalty of forfeiting two hundred pounds of tobacco, if he failed to vote. The sheriff was required to appoint five persons, and these persons, after being duly sworn, were required to enter the name of every candidate in a distinct column, and the name of every freeholder giving his vote, under the name of the person voted for, all of which was required to be done in the presence of the candidates or their agent, and upon the close of the polls the sheriff was ordered to proclaim the names of the successful candidates.

And it was further provided that any person who should directly or indirectly, except in his usual and ordinary course of hospitality, in his own house, give, present or allow to any person or persons, having voice or vote in such elections any money, gift, reward, or entertainment, or any promise, agreement, obligation or engagement, to any person, etc., "shall be declared guilty of bribery and corruption, and rendered incapable to sit, or vote, or to hold office."

Three Decisive Battles

Three Decisive Battles

ACCORDING to Sir Edward Creasy there have been only fifteen decisive battles in the world's history.

Dr. Douthat, in a lecture given at Bristol, claimed that the battle of Gettysburg was the sixteenth decisive battle of the world, his conclusion being that had the South won in this battle the United States would have been divided into three or more small countries, and, of course, would not have become a world power.

There are three important events in American history that may not be classed as decisive battles, yet they had an important part in the preservation of the Colonies and the acquisition of the great Northwest Territory. Historians allot very little space to these campaigns and the average student is apt to pass them by as of minor importance. The light of research has proved, however, that the frontiersmen of the Holston settlements carried to a successful conclusion three campaigns that were far-reaching in our struggle for independence. Elbert Hubbard says that the real hero is the quiet unostentatious soldier who carries "A Message to Garcia" without hope of reward or renown.

The valleys of the Holston River were settled by Scotch-Irish Presbyterians, who had struggled for a thousand years in their native highlands for religious and civil freedom. Inspired by this same patriotism they answered every call to go to the defense of their newly adopted country. Historians have not done justice to these brave frontiersmen from the fact that the number of men engaged in these expeditions was comparatively very small. The results, however, were far-reaching and of lasting importance.

Dunmore's War

The first of these events was known as Dunmore's War, which was really the beginning of the Revolution. There was only one battle fought in this war and but one regiment engaged by the Virginians. Prior to 1774, the Ohio confederation of Indians, consisting of Shawnees, Wyandottes, Mingoes and other tribes under the able leadership of Cornstalk, had been ravaging the frontier settlements west of the Blue Ridge Mountains. Some authorities think that Lord Dunmore was secretly in league with the Indians and encouraged their depredations, to distract attention from the oppressions of the royal government. These frequent incursions became so annoying that popular opinion forced the governor to take some action. Lord Dunmore finally mustered an army of men from the eastern settlements of Virginia. He also commissioned Colonel Andrew Lewis to enlist 1,500 men west of the Blue Ridge Mountains. At this time the county of Fincastle embraced all of the territory west of the Blue Ridge Mountains, extending to the Mississippi River. The Fincastle men were from Holston, Clinch, Watauga and New River settlements enlisted under the command of Colonel William Christian. The recruits from southwestern Virginia and eastern Tennessee were enlisted under Captains William Campbell, Daniel Smith and Evan Shelby. Colonel Lewis was instructed to proceed to Greenbrier Flats

(now Lewisburg, W. Va.) where he would
be joined by Lord Dunmore and his command. They were then to invade the Indian
territory and proceed against the towns
north of the Ohio River. Colonel Lewis
brought his men safely out of the wilderness
and camped at the junction of the Kanawha
and Ohio. They were attacked at sunrise on
the morning of October 10, by a force of
1,200 Indians under the leadership of Cornstalk. This is known as the battle of Point
Pleasant.

The Battle of Point Pleasant

It is generally conceded that the Indians
were in superior force; whether this be true
or not, they fought with unusual bravery
and ferocity. The battle lasted from daylight
until dark, after which the Indians crossed
the Ohio River and retreated to their own
towns. Colonel Lewis lost twenty per cent
of his entire regiment in killed and wounded,
but his men displayed the utmost courage
throughout the entire engagement. From
the standpoint of killed and wounded the
battle might be considered a draw, but in
far-reaching effect the advantage was de-

BATTLE OF KING'S MOUNTAIN

cidedly with the Colonies. First in importance, the frontiersmen here demonstrated that they had learned and adopted the Indian method of fighting and that they were more than a match for the red man at his own tactics. As soon as Lord Dunmore heard of the victory he crossed the Ohio River with his entire army and destroyed a number of the Indian towns as well as their crops. The defeat at Point Pleasant and this invasion of their own country had the effect of breaking their spirit and morale. Even the eloquence of Cornstalk could not persuade them to take the warpath again and the frontiers were not disturbed to any great extent for several years after the beginning of the Revolutionary War. This released the men of the Holston settlements to take part in such expeditions as the North Carolina campaign, which resulted in the victory of King's Mountain. The intimidation of the Ohio Indians also permitted the settling of Kentucky and the conquest of the Northwest by George Rogers Clark.

Battle of King's Mountain

The second event referred to was the battle of King's Mountain. Tarleton, with his

British dragoons, had been devastating the Carolinas and sweeping everything before him. Never had the cause of American independence looked more gloomy. Phillips with the faith of the true Highland Scotchman, crossed the Blue Ridge and made an appeal to his mountaineer cousins of the Holston settlements. These frontiersmen who had marched several hundred miles through the wilderness to meet Cornstalk's braves, quickly mobilized under Colonel Campbell and Shelby at Sapling Grove (now Bristol) to march against England's picked troops. They were joined at Sycamore Shoals by the Tennessee volunteers under the command of Colonel John Sevier. Dressed in homespun, wearing coonskin caps and armed with rifles, they presented a picturesque appearance. Their equipment consisted of powder horn and bullet pouch, with a measure of parched corn or meal for their sustenance. A considerable portion of the command were mounted, but the hardy footmen with their light equipment kept pace with the horses and arrived on the scene of the battle at the same time as the horsemen. Making a forced march across the mountains they learned

SURRENDER OF THE TROOPS
Commanded by Col Ferguson at
KINGS MOUNTAIN
7th October 1780.

EXPLANATION.

A. Col Shelby's Corps ....
B. Col Campbells ....
C. Col Sevier's ....
D. Maj Winston's ....
E. Col Hambrights ....
F. Maj Cleveland's ....
G. Col Cleveland's ....
H. Col Williams ....
I. Maj McDowel's ....
J. Browns Line previous
   to being surrounded.
K. Ditto in confusion.
L. Length of enemys
   encampment to Petros.
M. Col Ferguson's Grave
N. Monument of Colonel
   Cleveland & others.
O. Col Ferguson killed.
------- Route of the different Corps going into the Battle.

Engraved by W. Keenan Charleston S.C.
From a Drawing taken on the spot by Gentleman
For Ramsey's Annals of Tennessee.

that Colonel Ferguson was intrenched at King's Mountain, near the boundary line between the Carolinas. After a consultation of the officers, Colonel William Campbell was elected to command and it was decided to make an immediate attack. King's Mountain was surrounded by the little band of mountaineers, who advanced in Indian fashion, fighting from every tree and bush. So deadly was their aim, so determined was their purpose that the British forces were practically annihilated and Ferguson and many of his subordinates killed. Never was there a more decisive victory.

Just as the Indians had been checked in their rapacious raids on the north, so was Tarleton stopped in his Carolina career and forced to join Cornwallis at Yorktown. When Cornwallis heard the news that one of his choicest regiments had been destroyed by a band of mountaineers who fought with tomahawks and long rifles, his heart became as water and he surrendered to General Washington on Oct. 19, 1781. As the majority of the forces engaged were from the Holston settlements, they are entitled to the highest credit for this achievement

which directly led to the surrender of Cornwallis and the establishment of the first
great Republic. Thomas Jefferson, writing
from Monticello, Nov. 11, 1822, to Colonel
John Campbell in regard to the battle of
King's Mountain, said, "I remember well the
deep and grateful impression made on the
mind of everyone by that memorable victory.
It was the joyful annunciation of that turn
of the tide of success which terminated the
Revolutionary War, with the seal of our
Independence. The descendants of Colonel
Campbell may rest their heads quietly on
the pillow of his renown; history has conse-
crated and will forever preserve it in the
faithful annals of a grateful country." There
can be no higher authority quoted for our
claims that the frontiersmen from the Holston settlements struck the decisive blow in
the war for independence.

Conquest of the Northwest

The third expedition was the conquest of
the Northwest by George Rogers Clark and
his little band of frontiersmen from the
mountains of western Virginia and what is
now Tennessee and Kentucky.

SYCAMORE SHOALS TREATY

(From Mural Painting in State Capitol, Frankfort, Kentucky)

George Rogers Clark was born on his father's farm about two miles east of Charlottesville, Virginia, Nov. 19, 1752. He was of sturdy Scotch-Irish descent. His opportunity for securing an education at that date was very limited, but he had a mathematical mind and in some way learned surveying. He toured the Ohio Valley in 1772 and viewed what he considered the most beautiful country in the world. He accompanied Lord Dunmore on the Point Pleasant campaign, but was not actually in the battle, as Lord Dunmore's troops were some fifty miles away at Greenbrier Flats when the battle was fought. Clark was so impressed with the beauty and fertility of the Ohio Valley that he returned to Kentucky in 1775 and again in 1777, where he soon became a leader. At that time the state of Kentucky was a part of the state of Virginia and Clark was the first member of the Virginia legislature from the Kentucky settlements. He made the trip from Kentucky to Williamsburg through Cumberland Gap and via Bristol and Abingdon. He enlisted the support of Governor Patrick Henry and through his strong personality and unquestioned patriotism, was

granted five hundred pounds of gunpowder
for the defense of the Kentucky settlements.
By this act he cemented the Kentucky
frontiers to the Old Dominion.

He was opposed in his plans by Colonel
Arthur Campbell, the delegate from Washington County, who wanted to annex Kentucky to his county. In order to secure the
powder he was compelled to make a trip to
Pittsburgh, Penn., and then to float it down
the Ohio River on flatboats to the Kentucky
River, where it was taken inland and dis-
tributed to the settlements. Clark was very
silent and reserved, never sharing his confidence with any of his associates. With
almost prophetic vision he saw that the war
must be carried into the enemies' country
and the wonderful Northwest Territory
wrested from the British and Indians and
added to the federation of states which he
already felt was assured.

Colonel Hamilton in command of the
British forces, with headquarters at Fort
Dearborn, was continually inciting the
Indians to make incursions on the settle-
ments and encouraged the taking of scalps.
In the spring of 1777 Clark sent scouts into

SURRENDER OF THE TROOPS
Commanded by Col Ferguson at
KINGS MOUNTAIN
7th October 1780.

EXPLANATION.

A. Col Shelby's Corps
B. Col Campbells
C. Col Sevier's
D. Maj Winston's
E. Col Hambrights
F. Maj Chronicle's
G. Col Cleveland's
H. Col Williams
I. Maj McDowell's

J. Enemys Line previous
    to being surrounded.
K. Enemy in confusion
L. Length of enemy's
    encampment do Police
M. Col Fergusons Grave.
N. Monument of Colonel
    Chronicle & others.
O. Col Ferguson killed.
------ Route of the different Corps going into the Battle.

Engraved by W. Keenan Charleston S.C.
From a Drawing taken on the spot by Gen Graham
For Ramsey's Annals of Tennessee.

the Ohio territory to spy out the land and ascertain the possibilities of a campaign into the enemies' country. These scouts, like Joshua and Caleb, sent to spy out the Promised Land in the days of Moses, reported that the land was greatly to be desired, but the enemy were numerous and warlike.

Still keeping his own counsel, Clark returned to Virginia in the fall of 1777 to secure authority for his expedition. Once more he called on his friend, Governor Patrick Henry, and so magnetic was his appeal that he secured the cooperation of George Wythe, George Mason and Thomas Jefferson. They were all members of the council of defense and personally assumed responsibility for the funds incident to equipping the campaign. Twelve hundred pounds were advanced to Clark to finance his expedition and he was secretly empowered to raise seven companies of men west of the Blue Ridge. Considerable opposition was interposed to his recruiting and he succeeded in raising but four companies. They reached the falls of the Ohio in May, 1778, and camped on Corn Island in the midst of the Ohio River opposite what is now the city of Louisville.

A stockade was built on the island and the settlers moved to the south bank of the river a few months later and founded Louisville, which was named for our French ally. Here Clark made known to his little band of followers the true purpose of his expedition to wrest the territory north of the Ohio. In June, 1778, Clark embarked with his forces on flatboats and floated down the Ohio River. The exact date has been established by the astronomical fact that the sun went into total eclipse at the very moment that the boats were shooting the falls below Louisville. Such an event at this time was sufficient to have shed a gloom over the expedition which was going on so hazardous a mission.

The little flotilla landed at the mouth of the Tennessee River a few days later. Thence they marched overland and captured the town of Kaskaskia by stealth. This town, under British dominion, was garrisoned by French Creoles and commanded by Rochablave, a Frenchman. Clark displayed great sagacity in gaining the good will of the garrison and inhabitants and very soon won them over to the cause of American inde-

GEORGE ROGERS CLARK

pendence. He also proclaimed the principles of religious freedom, stating that "an American Commander has nothing to do with any church except to defend it from insult, and by the laws of the Republic, the Catholic religion had as great a privilege as any other." This tolerance completely won the Catholic priest Gibeault and his Creole followers and they remained loyal to the new Republic from that time.

A small detachment was sent against Cahokia, and with the assistance of his new friends, this place was quickly won over to the American cause. Vincennes was the next to fall under the spell of Clark's personality, Father Gibeault having volunteered to go with a few of his followers and win this strategic point to the cause of the Republic. This was accomplished and he returned in August leaving a small garrison of Clark's men to hold the fort. Clark now found himself in a very difficult position. He was in command of a territory larger than many of the European countries, surrounded on every side by hosts of savage Indians and threatened from the north by the British and the Indians from Canada.

He had only one hundred and seventy-five men and they were undisciplined and many of them were anxious to return home to their families. His tact and bravery in dealing with various Indian tribes did much to save his position.

Colonel Hamilton, the British commander at Detroit, had been planning an attack on Fort Pitt, but news of the capture of Vincennes forced him to change his plans. He immediately organized an expedition and on December 17 recaptured the town, although Captain Helms with two Americans made quite a show of defense. Had Hamilton pushed on he could easily have driven Clark out of Illinois at this time, but he waited in Vincennes believing that the rigors of winter would make him immune from attack. This was where he underestimated his adversary, Colonel Clark. In him he had an antagonist whose daring and bravery had not been equaled even on the frontier, where personal prowess was the rule and where men were trained to courage and hardihood by the ruthless forest warfare of the red men and their allies, the British. Clark decided to accomplish the impossible and make a

counterattack on Vincennes in the dead of
winter. At the head of a band of one hundred and seventy men, he set forth from
Kaskaskia on February 7. Their march was
two hundred and forty miles through a
trackless wilderness against a garrisoned
town with a strong fort defended by artillery. The first ten days of the march were
without insurmountable obstacles, but on
the twentieth rain set in, with accompany-
ing freshets in all of the streams that had to
be forded. The last twenty miles took six
days to accomplish. During this time the
men were practically without food and most
of the time waist deep in water. After the
most distressing hardships and privations
they succeeded in crossing the Wabash and
could overlook the fort from the heights
above the town. A surprise attack was
planned and executed just at nightfall. The
fort was surrounded and a sharp attack
made, which was renewed at daybreak.
After a brave show of resistance Colonel
Hamilton surrendered his garrison. Roosevelt says in his "Winning of the West," "In
truth it was a most notable achievement.
Clark had taken without artillery a heavy

stockade, protected by cannon and swivels and garrisoned by trained soldiers. Much credit belongs to Clark's men but most belongs to their leader. The boldness of his plan and the resolute skill with which he followed it out, his perseverance throughout the hardships of the midwinter march, the address with which he kept the French and Indians neutral and the masterful way in which he controlled his own troops, together with the ability and courage he displayed in the actual attack, combined to make his feat the most memorable of all of the deeds done west of the Alleghanies in the Revolutionary War."

It was likewise the most important in results, for had he been defeated the United States would not only have lost the Illinois territory but Kentucky as well.

With the capture of Vincennes, the Colonies secured a hold on the Northwest Territory that was never again relinquished. In the final treaty and settlement with Great Britain the right of possession was recognized and pressed to the utmost by our commissioners, led by John Jay. It is, of course, impossible to prove that but for the Virginia expedition under George Rogers Clark and his conquest, that the Ohio would have been made the boundary between the United States and Canada. But the old adage that possession is nine points of the law certainly had tremendous import in the settlement which gave to the Union the states of Kentucky, Ohio, Indiana, Illinois, Minnesota and Wisconsin. While the Indians kept up a running warfare for a number of years, Clark's campaign created such terror of his name that the Kentucky settlements were never again in actual danger of extermination.

To sum up the achievements of these men of the Holston settlements in the building of the nation would require the pen of a historian. Every descendant of these frontiersmen has a right to be proud of his heritage and to feel that this vast territory was won and preserved to the Union by the prowess of his forefathers. We are not a proud people, nor a boastful one, but if any section of this country has a right to be proud of its ancestors it is the Anglo-Saxon of the Holston Valleys and Appalachian highlands.

SKETCH TWELVE
Geology of the Kingsport District

Geology of the Kingsport District

THE geology of the Kingsport district is as interesting as any to be found in the world. Within less than one hundred miles are some of the oldest formations found in the earth's crust. Within fifty miles are the famous coal fields of southwestern Virginia and eastern Kentucky, while the Holston Valley contains many interesting caves and formations. The geological periods represented in the vicinity of Kingsport are:

1. Cambrian
2. Silurian
3. Devonian
4. Carboniferous
} Paleozoic

The geological history of the Kingsport region is extremely complicated even since the waters receded and it became dry land. All of the rocks appearing at the surface in this section are of sedimentary origin. They consist of sandstone, shale and limestone, having an average thickness of 17,000 feet, and representing great variety in composition and appearance. The materials of which they are composed were originally gravel, sand and mud derived from the waste of older rocks and from the remains of plants and animals which lived while the strata were being laid down. These rocks afford a record of almost uninterrupted sedimentation from early Cambrian to late Carboniferous times.

The wonderful coal seams of southwestern Virginia and eastern Kentucky were formed from deposits of peat or from buried vegetation. This would indicate at some remote age the presence of extensive swamps of either fresh or brackish water, in which flourished a luxuriant vegetation that was frequently buried by great washes of sand and mud. The sea in which the Paleozoic sediments were laid down covered most of the Appalachian section and the Mississippi Basin.

The oldest known rocks of this quadrangle were deposited in a trough or broad strait which was bounded on the east by the continental area then existing in the Smoky

Mountain and Blue Ridge region, and on the west by a land barrier which was probably somewhere in the western division of the Appalachian province, and which separated this trough from the great interior sea. Into this trough was swept the waste of the continental area to the east which, hardened into sandstone and shales, is now as the rocks of the lower Cambrian Age. The land forming the barrier west of the Appalachian Valley sank beneath the sea, and the coarse sediments of the preceding epoch gave place to an enormous and widespread limestone deposit which marks the close of the Cambrian and the beginning of Silurian time. This limestone presumably covers most, if not all, of the western division of the province and extends eastward to the base of the Appalachian Mountains. From the proximity of this outcrop to the supposed shore line of that period it seems probable that the land area to the east was practically at base level and that no coarse sediments were delivered to the Appalachian sea from that quarter. In early Silurian time this land area was elevated and such quantities of sand and mud were swept into the sea that the formation of limestone was interrupted near the shore, but farther out it continued to form for some time. Finally, however, the sea became too muddy for the formation of limestone except in central Kentucky and Tennessee, and the entire Appalachian Valley was covered with a thick deposit of shale. The land continued to rise and the shore line migrated across the Appalachian Valley, leaving a heavy deposit of clean beach sand to mark its progress. Near the close of Silurian time there was an upward movement along the Cincinnati Arch, making this a land area from which some of the older formations were removed by erosion. A slight subsidence allowed the next succeeding formation to be spread as a thin veneer over this eroded surface.

During the Devonian time the Kingsport quadrangle was doubtless covered by the sea which extended over most of the Appalachian province. In the earlier stage of this period the land to the east of the Paleozoic sea was probably near base level, but in the closing stage the land in the northeastern part of the United States was greatly elevated, and from this were swept immense

DANIEL BOONE ELM AND OLD SILK MILL ON NORTH FORK OF HOLSTON RIVER
AT ROTHERWOOD

quantities of sandy waste which were spread as far south as this region.

The beginning of the Carboniferous time is marked by marine conditions which permitted the formation of a great wedge of limestone extending from southern Pennsylvania and Ohio to the southern extremity of the province. Following the period of limestone deposition came an uprising of the crust of the earth which produced a shallow sea and moderately high land in the immediate vicinity, from which large quantities of sandy waste were poured into the waters of the sea and mingled with the calcareous material that accumulated there from time to time. Apparently many alterations of level took place in the early part of this period, which resulted in the deposition of beds of very diverse characteristics.

Finally, marine conditions passed away and the deposition of the coal-bearing rocks took place in fresh or brackish water basins in which coal plants flourished from time to time, and in which accumulated the peat that in after ages was altered into coal. At first the coal basin consisted of a narrow trough occupying the southeastern margin of the present field, and in that trough the earliest seams of coal were deposited. With the increased load of sediments poured into this basin came further subsidence and the encroachment of the waters of the basin toward the northwest, upon a land area that, in a general way, occupied the Cincinnati Arch. The continued subsidence of this basin permitted the accumulation of coal-bearing rocks over a wider and wider territory, until finally it reached the present proportions of the coal field and probably extended some distance beyond. In the later stages of the Carboniferous period the conditions must have changed materially, for the sediments consist of red and green shales of very fine texture, interbedded, curiously enough, with coarse sandstones and heavy conglomerates. The origin of these red shales is still a matter of doubt, but it is evident that they represent peculiar conditions, which would make an interesting chapter in the geologic history of this region if the conditions could be rightly interpreted from the sediments as they occur to-day.

Finally this basin was elevated above the water level and the Appalachian coal field was added to the continental area of North America. This extensive coal field has brought prosperity to this section by furnishing cheap fuel to the numerous industries at Kingsport and throughout the length and breadth of the Holston Valleys.

The Unaka National Forest

The Unaka National Forest

ONE of the most attractive scenic sections of the Kingsport District is the Unaka National Forest. It can easily be reached in one hour's ride from Kingsport over a splendid concrete highway. This beautiful tract of mountain valleys and upland now embraces 190,000 acres of land in Federal ownership, and will ultimately contain approximately half a million acres of forest land. A considerable portion of the forest is within the limits of Tennessee and embraces a portion of Sullivan County. The forest derives its name from the Cherokee word "Unaka" meaning "white clay," in allusion to the kaolin deposits found in the region of Erwin, Tennessee. Extensive potteries have been erected in this section and high grade ceramics are manufactured. The entire Holston and Iron Mountains are within the Unaka Forest boundary. On the southern portion of the forest are the Unaka and Bald Mountains. Mount Rogers (altitude 5,719 feet) and White Top Mountain (altitude 5,520 feet) the two highest peaks in Virginia, are in the Unaka National Forest.

The Nolichucky, Doe and Watauga rivers flow through the southern portion of the forest, while the Holston parallels it on the northwest. The Lee Highway, the southern transcontinental highway route from Washington, D. C., to San Francisco, California, skirts the Unaka National Forest for a distance of nearly one hundred miles to the Tennessee border at Bristol. The region in which the Unaka National Forest lies forms the eastern boundary of the Holston Valley. This valley possesses a very dramatic history and its pioneers and their descendants have had no small part in the building of the nation.

The Unaka National Forest has a twofold duty: first, to supply the local wood-using industries with a portion of their raw material; second, to be a vast playground for all of those who wish to use and enjoy it. The forest in its primitive state was a paradise for game of all descriptions. The Chero-

kees, Shawnees, Chickasaws, Chickamaugas, Creeks and Catawbas frequently entered its boundaries on their hunting expeditions.

The "Overhill" Cherokees, a subdivision of the main nation, dwelt in the present confines of the Unaka National Forest. They were reputed to be one of the most warlike tribes of the southern Indians.

The soldiers from eastern Tennessee and southwestern Virginia mobilized at Sycamore Shoals, near Elizabethton, Tennessee, before starting on their journey across the mountains to wrest the Carolinas from the dominion of the British General Tarleton (Oct. 7, 1780).

The route followed by these frontiersmen led up Doe River, between Roan and Yellow Mountains and on to King's Mountain.

Daniel Boone erected a cabin and dwelt for a number of years in what is now the Unaka National Forest. In 1760 he explored the Holston and Clinch River valleys. All of his routes crossed territory now embraced in the Unaka National Forest. One route lay through what is now Shouns and Mountain City, Tennessee, over the Iron Mountains across Shady Valley, then over the

Holston Mountains to Fish Dam on the
Holston River.   Another route followed
through Taylor's Valley, Virginia and across
to the Holston River, through what is now
Abingdon, Virginia. Again he came down
Roan Creek, through what is now Butler,
Tennessee, thence down the Watauga to
Long Island, the present site of Kingsport.
Other routes said to have been taken by
Boone were down the Watauga, Doe and
Nolichucky rivers. All of these routes
passed through what is now the Unaka
National Forest and converged at Cumber-
land Gap, the gateway to Kentucky.

Originally the area which is now the
Unaka National Forest contained the finest
stands of hardwood timber in the Appalachian highlands. Due to the influence of
altitude the Unaka National Forest contains
a greater variety of species than any other
forest region in the entire United States.

The mountains in the Unaka National
Forest are said by geologists to be entirely
the work of long erosion in some of the
oldest rock formations in the United States.
There is no evidence of semirecent cata-
clysmic action.

DANIEL BOONE'S FIRST VIEW OF KENTUCKY FROM THE CUMBERLAND MOUNTAINS
(From Mural Painting in State Capitol, Frankfort, Kentucky)

Commercial quantities of iron and manganese and some silver and gold have been found in the area now in the Unaka National Forest. Ruins of many charcoal iron furnaces are still to be found. The product of these old furnaces was far superior to iron made in the modern blast furnaces. The iron made in these furnaces was hauled to Kingsport and transported down the Holston, Tennessee and Mississippi rivers to New Orleans. To provide charcoal for the operation of these old furnaces great areas of forest lands were cut over and this operation was followed by forest fires. Large stretches of forest lands were also cut over by commercial operations in the most wasteful manner. The waste material was burned and the young timber, left standing, thereby destroyed. Had fire been kept out of the cut-over sections an excellent stand of timber would now occupy the area. The mountains of the forest area are steep and only valuable for watershed protection and timber production. Fire has ever been "the scourge of the forest." Forest fires drove out the game, destroyed their young and above all their food supply. In Unaka National Forest the resources are protected but not locked up permanently. Forest resources are timber, grass, fish and game, water supplies, minerals and the use of the forest for recreation. As rapidly as funds become available the Forest Service is developing public camp grounds. Locations for summer homes in the forest area are also granted to desirable citizens at a nominal cost. The Unaka National Forest is for the perpetual use of all who do not abuse it. The establishment of the National Forests was one of the wisest acts of legislation ever put on our statute books. They will continue to grow in beauty and usefulness for centuries to come and in time will be restored to their primitive grandeur.

The Camp Meeting

SKETCH FOURTEEN

The Camp Meeting

METHODISM was introduced into the United States in 1766 but did not become established in Sullivan County, Tenn., until 1774. The first Methodist organization was convened at the home of Edward Cox near Bluff City, Tenn. This was the first organization to be formed in Sullivan County or in the state of Tennessee. The first conference of the Methodist church ever held in this section assembled at Cawoods on the Holston River in April, 1788. The first Methodist church in Washington County, Virginia, was erected in Abingdon in the spring of 1823. Rev. John Tevis, of the Kentucky conference, was placed in charge of the Holston district in 1820. The confines of the Holston district comprised more than nine hundred square miles at that time. In the early part of the nineteenth century there were very few Methodists in this vast territory and the labors of a pre-

165

siding elder were very onerous indeed. His duties consisted in preaching two sermons every day, riding horseback from one meeting to the next, making personal visitations to the sick, cheering up the despondent, burying the dead, besides attending the regular quarterly meetings. The camp meeting took the place of the modern revival in the spiritual life of the pioneers. It was the occasion of a great reunion and love feast for the Methodists, and many of them came from great distances and even from adjoining states to attend these annual occasions.

The camp meeting had a very important part in the spiritual life of the early settlers. A graphic description of the old time camp meeting is found in the autobiography of Mrs. Julia A. Tevis, "Sixty Years in a School-room," which is reproduced as follows:

In September, 1823, the annual camp meeting was held near the Sulphur Springs, in Smyth County, Virginia. A beautiful grove of grand old trees in a lovely mountain gorge marked the spot that had, for this special purpose, been donated to the Methodists for the term of one hundred years by Colonel Thompson, the son-in-law of Mother Russell. The camp meetings held on this spot were widely diffusive of good, and were really necessary in a country so sparsely settled as this was at that time.

[Her story continues]: We reached the camp ground late in the evening of a brilliant autumn day, while yet flakes of sunshine, sifting through the pendant branches, fell like tremulous gleaming gems upon the heads of the assembled congregation. Near by but hidden under the foliage of the water willow, was a spring widening into smooth, deep water—a miniature lake, throwing back the sunshine like a mirror, and keeping all its secret depths unlighted; then contracting into a narrow stream, it ran, glittering like a silver thread, through the valley beneath. Beyond it rose a magnificent mountain, skirted with woods and dotted with farms to the very summit. The declining sun touched everything with a soft and tender light, and the few fleecy clouds, visible in the fathomless blue air, seemed like white doves of peace, floating with wings outspread in benediction over the assembled multitude of God's people, who had come up into the wilderness, apart from the dust and heat and hurry of existence that they might hold sweet communion with each other, and bow with united hearts before their great Creator, here to worship Him under the overarching skies in a "Temple Not Made With Hands."

A winding pathway up the mountain side, quite concealed from the passers-by, led to a spot high up, where, under the spreading oak and chestnut, prayer was offered during the intervals of public preaching for earnest seekers of religion. Pious and experienced women, who were ever laboring for the good of souls, were accustomed to pray there with and for the female penitents and seekers of religion. All along its steep ascent were quiet nooks and shady dells where no prying eye or careless footstep would be likely to intrude.

My first night at the encampment was full of beauty. At each of the four corners of the camp-ground was left the stump of a large tree, four or five feet high, the tops of which were rendered fire-proof by a layer of brick and mortar, and upon these blazed burning pine knots, lighting up all the sur-roundings with their tall flames. Among the dark green foliage glittered the flickering lights of numer-ous lamps attached to trees; beautiful white vapors floated in the starlit sky, now resting an instant, then glancing onward, hiding the face of the full moon like a snowy veil, cast over the jeweled brow of a queen. In the stand were reverend, good-looking men, whose very appearance inspired confidence. The trumpet was sounded and long lines of people were seen wending their way to roughly constructed seats, made for the occasion. I never saw more perfect order, more attention to politeness and decorum, in any assemblage of people. The hymn was announced— all sang together; in those days singing was worship— the beginning, as it were, of prayer. The assembled multitude rose up to sing, and after repeating the last two lines of the hymn, fell upon their knees to con-tinue that act of devotion in prayer; and there was power in it, felt by all. When we rose again a well-known melody poured forth from the hearts of the whole congregation, full of freedom, of simplicity, of feeling and energetic sentiment. It was as the wings of seraphim, upon which the assembled multitude were borne heavenward, thus elevating preachers and hearers in the introductory, so that the whole subse-quent service showed its effect. Never did truer music gush from the human heart; and a more efficacious means for inspiring the minds of the hearers with the love of religion could hardly be conceived than when its sublime sentiments are clothed in sweet musical harmony that captivates the senses and touches the soul through the medium of the ear and heart. Many of the old tunes, habitual in the worship of those days, seem instinctive to the devotional feeling of our people. Charles Wesley's hymns, so full of glowing piety, would kindle a heavenly flame in the hearts of any assembly sincerely desirous of praising and worshipping God. The fact is, the Methodist singing, at church and at home, once had a charm of its own— and everybody liked it, because it made melody in every heart. Our surroundings were favorable to devotion. We were too remote from cities and towns to be annoyed by the curious and idle. Even those who came to observe and be observed remained to pray. Public services never continued later than ten o'clock P. M.—at that hour all were expected to seek repose; yet in some of the tents the voice of prayer and praise was heard at a much later hour, and at intervals, the prolonged shouts of happy souls. The sound of the trumpet at early dawn awakened all slumberers for morning prayer, after which a frugal meal—nothing hot but tea or coffee, was prepared, and then an interval of two or three hours spent in private devotion before the eleven o'clock preaching. We dined at precisely one o'clock, giving an opportunity for the serious and pentinent to withdraw again for private prayer.

The Jacksons in Sullivan

The Jacksons in Sullivan

SULLIVAN COUNTY, Tenn., has had many distinguished sons and daughters who were natives of the county. There have been many others of like prominence who have dwelt within the borders of the county for a long time and then passed on to other fields of endeavor. Two of these sojourners stand out in bold relief and it is an interesting coincidence that their lives afterwards became linked and they participated in some of the most dramatic events that have ever taken place on the continent. While the date is not accurately known, it is an accepted fact that Andrew Jackson resided or boarded with the family of William Cobb in the "Forks of the Holston" in Sullivan County, Tenn., only a few miles from Kingsport. At this time Andrew was a rollicking young attorney, who had already shown his daring spirit in an encounter with a British officer in North Carolina.

He attended court at Abingdon and Jonesboro, at the latter place he was admitted to the bar in 1788 and also sat as one of the magistrates of the county court. His signature may be found on the records of the clerk's office at that place.

In the fall of 1779 Colonel John Donelson brought his family from Virginia and settled near Long Island (Kingsport). Colonel Donelson was a prominent surveyor and had rendered valuable service in negotiating treaties with the Indians.

Glowing reports of the beautiful Cumberland Valleys had been brought back to the Holston settlements by the explorers. Fired by these reports of the beauty of the country and the fertility of the soil Colonel Donelson conceived the most daring plan that had yet been made to settle the Cumberland Valley. Building a flotilla of thirty flatboats he and others embarked on Dec. 22, 1779, on this hazardous voyage down the Holston and Tennessee Rivers.

There were about three hundred persons in the party and in the roster of names may be found some of the most prominent pioneer families of Tennessee and Kentucky. With

RACHEL DONELSON
(MRS. ANDREW JACKSON)

Colonel Donelson's party was his young
daughter Rachel, only thirteen years of age.
This young girl bore her part of the hardships of the voyage and early displayed
those beautiful traits of character which
made her the wife of Andrew Jackson a few
years later. Rachel Donelson's influence over
Jackson's fiery nature was very marked and
his love for her grew with the passing years.
Tennessee has always been proud of Rachel
Jackson. Her life and character have been
an example to the women of the state. The
breath of scandal has never been able to
diminish the luster of her purity and good-
ness. Sullivan County rejoices that she once
lived within its borders. The city of Kingsport proudly records that it was from this
point that Rachel Donelson embarked on the
voyage that was to make her the wife of
Andrew Jackson and consort of a president
of the United States. Oliver Taylor says in
"Historic Sullivan:" "Rachel Jackson was
a type of Tennessee frontierswoman whose
culture and refinement influenced the times."

Rachel Jackson was not versed in the arts,
wiles and social usuages of the society of the
eighteenth century. She did not have the

classical education available to the favored
few in those pioneer days. But she had a
heart of gold that could pour itself out in
love and sympathy for others, even unto the
lowliest slave on her plantation. She had
"that something," a spiritual side to her
character that doesn't count for much with
some folks nowadays. She had the good,
old-fashioned religion and ever kept the fear
of God in her heart. If she was plain, she
was the very highest type of the noble
frontierwomen who so bravely did their part
in subduing the wilderness and winning the
great western empire. A visit to her lovely
old mansion, "The Hermitage," is almost
like being transported into a bygone past.
It is like visiting a shrine from which arises
sweet incense. Evidences of refinement and
culture are seen on every hand. There is no
colonial mansion in the Southland more
truly representative of the culture and refinement of the old South than The Hermitage.

Rachel Donelson may have lacked some
of the superficial culture of the twentieth
century, yet Lafayette, the prince of patri-
cians, made a journey of nearly a thousand
miles to visit in her home. It is true her

life was lived amid stern and stormy events and she was witness to many turbulent scenes, but nothing that may be written will detract from the love that is borne for her in the heart of every true Southerner.

The South has always been proud of its beautiful and noble women, but of Rachel Donelson it can truly be said, "Many daughters have done virtuously, but thou excellest them all."

Frontier Roads

Frontier Roads

THE first settlers of the Shenandoah Valley came from the neighborhood of Philadelphia, Penn. They followed either a buffalo or Indian trail to the head of the Shenandoah Valley near Winchester, Va. Finding this the most beautiful section of the new country yet explored the Scotch-Irish and German settlers from Pennsylvania continued to migrate to Virginia in increasing numbers.

From 1740 until the Revolutionary War this migration continued, many of the hardy frontiersmen pushing on down the Holston Valley into the Cumberland settlements of Tennessee and through Cumberland Gap into Kentucky. A well defined buffalo trail extended from Harpers Ferry down the Shenandoah Valley to Big Lick (Roanoke), Va., thence westward to the headwaters of the Holston River, thence following the Holston Valley to Long Island (Kingsport) and from this point through southwestern Virginia to Cumberland Gap and on into Kentucky. In this day of rapid progress and educational advantages we are apt to belittle the ability and knowledge of the pioneers of this section. Some of their achievements, however, were equal to the best engineering feats of the twentieth century. As early as 1760 Colonel William Byrd cut out a road following the old buffalo trail from Big Lick, Va. (Roanoke), to Long Island (Kingsport). Over this route he took an army of six hundred men with supplies to the relief of Fort Loudon, Tenn., which was besieged by the Cherokee Indians. Practically all of the early settlers of southwestern Virginia, eastern Tennessee and Kentucky passed over this route in search of their new homes. The Lee Highway, leading from Washington, D. C., to the Pacific coast, follows this old route for more than two hundred miles. The early frontiersmen were not entirely ignorant of the advantages of good roads and accurate information in regard to them. In the year 1784 John Filson published a history of Kentucky and at the conclusion of the book the Road Log on page facing 182 was given.

ROAD from Philadelpia to the Falls of the Ohio by land.

	M	M.D
FROM Philadelphia to Lancaster	66	
To Wright's on Sufquehannah	10	76
To York-town	12	88
Abbott's-town	15	103
Hunter's-town	10	113
the mountain at Black's Gap	3	116
the other fide of the mountain	7	123
the Stone-houfe Tavern	25	148
Wadkin's Ferry on Potowmack	14	162
Martinburg	13	175
Winchefter	20	195
Newtown	8	203
Stover's-town	10	213
Woodftock	12	225
Shanandoah River	15	240
the North branch of Shanandoah	29	269
Stanton	15	284
the North Fork of James River	37	321
James River	18	339
Boterourt Court-houfe	12	351
Woods's on Catauba River	21	372
Patterfon's on Roanoak	9	381
the Allegany Mountain	8	389
New River	12	401
the forks of the road	16	417
P		To

FALLS OF THE OHIO—*Louisville, Ky.*
NEW RIVER—*Radford.*

	M	M.D
To Fort Chiffel	12	429
a Stone Mill	11	440
Boyd's	8	448
head of Holftein	5	453
Wafhington Court-houfe	45	498
the Block-houfe	35	533
Powel's Mountain	33	566
Walden's Ridge	3	569
the Valley Station	4	573
Martin Cabbin's	25	598
Cumberland Mountain	20	618
the ford of Cumberland River	13	631
the Flat Lick	9	640
Stinking Creek	2	642
Richland Creek	7	649
Down Richland Creek	8	657
Rackoon Spring	6	663
Laurel River	2	665
Hazle Patch	15	680
the ford on Rock-Caftle River	10	690
English's Station	25	715
Col. Edwards's at Crab-Orchard	3	718
Whitley's Station	5	723
Logan's Station	5	728
Clark's Station	7	735
Crow's Station	4	739
Harrol's Station	3	742
Harand's	4	746
		To

FORT CHISFEL—*Max Meadows.*
BOYD'S—*Wytheville.*
HEAD OF HOLSTEIN—*Marion.*
WASHINGTON COURT HOUSE—*Abingdon.*
THE BLOCK HOUSE—*Kingsport.*

	M	M.D
To Harbifon's	10	756
Bard's-town	25	781
the Salt-works	25	806
the Falls of the Ohio	20	826

Kentucke is fituated about South, 60° Weft from Philadelphia, and, on a ftraight line, may be about fix hundred miles diftant from that city.

ROAD to Pittfburg, and Diftances from thence down the Ohio River to its mouth, and from thence down the Miffiffippi to the Mexican Gulph.

	M	M.D
FROM Philadelphia to Lan- cafter	66	
To Middletown	26	92
Harris's Ferry	10	102
Carlifle	17	119
Shippenburgh	21	140
Chamber's-town	11	151
Fort Loudon	13	164
Fort Littleton	18	182
Juniata Creek	19	201
		To

FALLS OF THE OHIO—*Louisville, Ky.*

The distance between points and the total
mileage check with the mileage given in the
Blue Book of 1926, with very slight varia-
tion. The route given in this Log is followed
closely by the National Highways leading
out of Philadelphia to Lancaster, Pa., thence
via Winchester and the Lee Highway to
Kingsport; from this point via route ten
through Cumberland Gap, thence via the
Dixie Highway to the Falls of the Ohio
(modern Louisville). There is not a route in
the entire country that is more replete with
history than the Lee Highway. Over this
old trail marched the army of Colonel
William Byrd in 1760 to the relief of Fort
Loudon. In 1774 Colonel Andrew Lewis
mobilized a regiment of 1,200 frontiersmen
and traveled over it on his famous campaign
against the Ohio Indians. In 1776 Colonel
William Christian collected his little army
from southwestern Virginia and invaded the
Cherokee country on the southern border of
Tennessee, again using the old buffalo trail
as a military highway. In 1774 Captain John
Montgomery raised a company of men west
of the Blue Ridge Mountains and accompanied George Rogers Clark in his conquest

of the Northwest Territory. The route followed, from southwestern Virginia to the Falls of the Ohio, was the same as shown on Filson's old Log. In 1780 Colonel Willaim Campbell mustered his men from the far reaches of Washington County and marched his small army to Shelby's Fort (Bristol), and thence on to King's Mountain and victory. Until the completion of the railroad in 1855, from Harpers Ferry, Va., to Bristol, Tenn., this old route described by Filson was one of the most important thoroughfares in the entire country.

With the coming of the railroads the highways ceased to be of service for long distance traveling and gradually their importance decreased. With the beginning of the twentieth century came the automobile age and the demand for good roads. Twenty-five years later the tourist can start from Philadelphia, follow the old Filson Log and in three days of moderate driving be in Louisville, Ky., a total distance of 825 miles, practically the entire route being substantial, hard-surfaced road, the section from Bristol to Kingsport, twenty-five miles, being of concrete construction twenty feet wide and

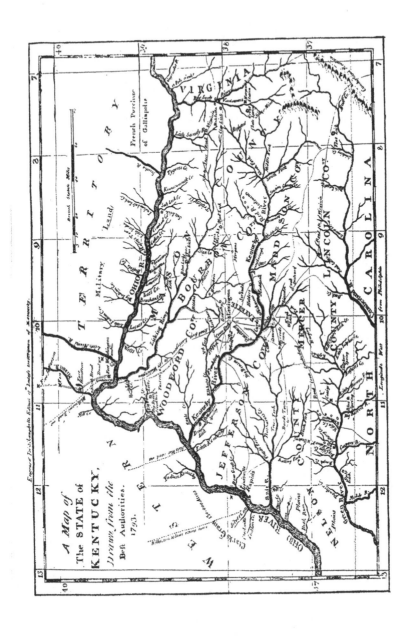

A Map of The STATE of KENTUCKY, Drawn from the Best Authorities. 1793.

one of the most picturesque roads in all this mountain district.

When Colonel William Byrd cut out a road from eastern Virginia to Long Island (Kingsport) in 1760, the route from the Kingsport settlements to Kentucky was still but a buffalo trail impassable for wagons until fifteen years later.

In 1775 the Transylvania Company purchased from the Cherokee Indians large boundaries of land in Kentucky. This purchase was ratified by the Cherokees at the Treaty of Sycamore Shoals, near Elizabethton, Tenn. To make this purchase available to settlers Daniel Boone was employed by the Transylvania Company to open a route from Long Island (Kingsport) through Cumberland Gap into Kentucky. The building of the Wilderness Road was begun March 10, 1775. No cheering crowds were present, no brass bands pealed forth, no flags or banners floated on the breeze, at the beginning of this historical undertaking or when the pioneer axmen had severed the last sapling on the Kentucky side. Little did Daniel Boone dream that he was building a road that opened the way for the conquest of an empire, that would be the ultimate means of adding seven great states to the Union; that he was opening a route over which countless men, women and even little children would pass to carve out a home in this primitive wilderness and to found a great commonwealth, not as British vassals but as free American citizens.

INDEX

ACKERMANN, Nick 13
ALLEN, Hugh 72
ANDERSON, John 37 38 91
    John Jr 38 William 48
ANNE, Queen 23
ANTRIM, Earl of 21
ARBUCKLE, Capt 71
AVERY, Waighstill 56
BANCE, Lt 72
BELL, ---- 24
BLACKBURN, Gideon 6
BLAIR, ---- 24
BLAND, Richard 101
BLEDSOE, Anthony 37 53 55
    81 Isaac 51
BOGGS, Hobert 51
BOONE, ---- 65 160 Daniel 15
    66 159 185 James 66
BOQUET, ---- 63
BRAKIN, Mathew 72
BRECKENRIDGE, ---- 24
BROWN, ---- 24
BUCHANAN, ---- 18 John 33
    William 81
BUFORD, Thos 72
BYRD, Col 47 48
    William 46 182 183 185
CABOT, ---- 15
CAESAR, ---- 27
CAGE, William 91

CAMERON, ---- 53
    Alexander 77
CAMPBELL, ---- 24 Arthur
    88 89 91 100 136 Charles
    33 Col 89 132 David 88 91
    100 John 51 81 134
    William 68 83 100 129
    133 184
CARMACK, Mr 72
CARTER, Landon 91
CASWELL, Gov 37 96
CATLIN, George 11
CHAPMAN, Thomas 91
CHARLES I, 20
CHISWELL, John 47
CHRISTIAN, ---- 51 Col 54
    55 Gilbert 37 48 William
    51 52 56 68 83 100 129
    183
CLARK, ---- 136 137 138 139
    141 142 Col 140 George
    Rogers 15 131 134 135
    143 183 Henry 37 Nathan
    37
COBB, William 173
COCKE, William 37 52 79 81
    92
COLUMBA, ---- 19
COLUMBUS, ---- 15
CONISTON, Joseph 56

187

188

189

Made in the USA
Las Vegas, NV
08 April 2022

47088939R00138